Sense and Respond Logistics

Integrating Prediction, Responsiveness, and Control Capabilities

Robert S. Tripp, Mahyar A. Amouzegar, Ronald G. McGarvey,
Rick Bereit, David George, Joan Cornuet

Prepared for the United States Air Force
Approved for public release; distribution unlimited

PROJECT AIR FORCE

The research reported here was sponsored by the United States Air Force under Contract F49642-01-C-0003. Further information may be obtained from the Strategic Planning Division, Directorate of Plans, Hq USAF.

Library of Congress Cataloging-in-Publication Data

Tripp, Robert S., 1944–
    Sense and respond logistics : integrating prediction, responsiveness, and control capabilities / Robert S. Tripp, Mahyar A. Amouzegar, [et al.].
      p. cm.
    "MG-488."
    Includes bibliographical references.
    ISBN-13: 978-0-8330-3978-1 (pbk. : alk. paper)
    1. United States. Air Force—Supplies and stores. 2 Command and control systems—United States. 3. Airlift, Military—United States. 4. Deployment (Strategy) I. Amouzegar, Mahyar A. II. McGarvey, Ronald G. III. Title.

UG1103.T75 2006
358.4'1411—dc22

                                                                    2006024048

The RAND Corporation is a nonprofit research organization providing objective analysis and effective solutions that address the challenges facing the public and private sectors around the world. RAND's publications do not necessarily reflect the opinions of its research clients and sponsors.

RAND® is a registered trademark.

Cover photo courtesy of the Integrator

Published 2006 by the RAND Corporation
1776 Main Street, P.O. Box 2138, Santa Monica, CA 90407-2138
1200 South Hayes Street, Arlington, VA 22202-5050
4570 Fifth Avenue, Suite 600, Pittsburgh, PA 15213-2665
RAND URL: http://www.rand.org/
To order RAND documents or to obtain additional information, contact
Distribution Services: Telephone: (310) 451-7002;
Fax: (310) 451-6915; Email: order@rand.org

Preface

This monograph discusses U.S. Air Force progress toward implementing sense and respond logistics (S&RL) or, as defined more broadly in this monograph, sense and respond combat support (S&RCS). As the United States and the Department of Defense transition current forces to a fighting force tailored to the new challenges of the 21st century, responsiveness and flexibility have become fundamental qualities in operational and support forces. Combat support (CS) personnel have traditionally not been integrated into the operational planning cycle and have developed support plans only after the operational plan has been established. To succeed in their task of supplying essential support materials to operational forces engaged in combat or humanitarian missions, CS forces developed consumption formulas and models, based on relatively long supply chains, that often failed to accurately predict support needs. To compensate for possible deficiencies in the estimates and the relatively long resupply times, they sent "mountains of supplies" to the war zone to ensure that there would be enough materiel to cover the resupply times.

These "just-in-case" approaches have been noted by the military, and more responsive and adaptive approaches have been the subject of a good deal of study. This monograph describes some of the research that has been conducted on the military CS system, focusing on improvements in prediction capabilities, responsiveness of supply chains, and a governing command and control system. Progress has been made in all three areas, and these results have improved Air Force ability to respond to the unique challenges of national defense in the new century. Even so, much remains to be done in the transformation of Air Force CS processes to meet the requirements needed to enable S&RCS capabilities.

This monograph tracks this progress, explains the challenges, and plots critical requirements to develop an effective system—one that senses what is happening on the battlefield and responds to actual requirements rapidly.

The research reported here was sponsored by the Deputy Chief of Staff for Installations and Logistics, U.S. Air Force (A4/7, formerly AF/IL), and conducted within the Resource Management Program of RAND Project AIR FORCE. It should be of interest to logisticians, operators, and planners throughout the Department of Defense, especially those in the Air Force.

This monograph is one of a series of RAND Corporation reports that address agile combat support (ACS) options. Other publications issued as part of the Supporting Air and Space Expeditionary Forces series include the following:

- *An Integrated Strategic Agile Combat Support Planning Framework*, Robert S. Tripp, Lionel A. Galway, Paul S. Killingsworth, et al. (MR-1056-AF). This report describes an integrated combat support planning framework that may be used to evaluate support options on a continuing basis, particularly as technology, force structure, and threats change.
- *New Agile Combat Support Postures*, Lionel A. Galway, Robert S. Tripp, et al. (MR-1075-AF). This report describes how alternative resourcing of forward operating locations (FOLs) can support employment timelines for future Air and Space Expeditionary Forces (AEF) operations. It finds that rapid employment for combat requires some prepositioning of resources at FOLs.
- *An Analysis of F-15 Avionics Options*, Eric Peltz et al. (MR-1174-AF). This report examines alternatives for meeting F-15 avionics maintenance requirements across a range of likely scenarios. The authors evaluate investments for new F-15 Avionics Intermediate Shop test equipment against several support options, including

deploying maintenance capabilities with units, performing maintenance at forward support locations (FSLs), and performing all maintenance at the home station for deploying units.

- *A Concept for Evolving to the Agile Combat Support/Mobility System of the Future,* Robert S. Tripp, Lionel A. Galway, Timothy L. Ramey, et al. (MR-1179-AF). This report describes the vision for the ACS system of the future based on individual commodity study results.
- *Expanded Analysis of LANTIRN Options,* Amatzia Feinberg et al. (MR-1225-AF). This report examines alternatives for meeting Low Altitude Navigation and Targeting Infrared for Night (LANTIRN) support requirements for AEF operations. The authors evaluate investments for new LANTIRN test equipment against several support options, including deploying maintenance capabilities with units, performing maintenance at FSLs, or performing all maintenance at support hubs in the Continental United States for deploying units.
- *Alternatives for Jet Engine Intermediate Maintenance,* Mahyar A. Amouzegar, Lionel A. Galway, and Amanda Geller (MR-1431-AF). This report evaluates the manner in which Jet Engine Intermediate Maintenance (JEIM) shops can best be configured to facilitate overseas deployments. The authors examine a number of JEIM support options, which are distinguished primarily by the degree to which JEIM support is centralized or decentralized. See also *Engine Maintenance Systems Evaluation (Enmasse): A User's Guide,* Mahyar A. Amouzegar and Lionel A. Galway (MR-1614-AF).
- *An Operational Architecture for Combat Support Execution Planning and Control,* James Leftwich et al. (MR-1536-AF). This report outlines the framework for evaluating options for combat support execution planning and control. The analysis describes the combat support command and control operational architecture as it is now and as it should be in the future. It also describes the changes that must take place to achieve that future state.
- *Reconfiguring Footprint to Speed Expeditionary Aerospace Forces Deployment,* Lionel A. Galway, Mahyar A. Amouzegar, et al.

(MR-1625-AF). This report develops an analysis framework—as a footprint configuration—to assist in devising and evaluating strategies for footprint reduction. The authors attempt to define footprint and to establish a way to monitor its reduction.

- *Analysis of Maintenance Forward Support Location Operations,* Amanda Geller et al. (MG-151-AF). This monograph discusses the conceptual development and recent implementation of maintenance forward support locations (also known as centralized intermediate repair facilities [CIRFs]) for the U.S. Air Force. The analysis focuses on the years leading up to and including the A4/7 (formerly AF/IL) CIRF test, which tested the operations of centralized intermediate repair facilities in the European theater from September 2001 to February 2002.

- *Lessons from Operation Enduring Freedom,* Robert S. Tripp, Kristin F. Lynch, et al. (MR-1819-AF). This report analyzes combat support experiences associated with Operation Enduring Freedom and compares them with those associated with Operation Allied Force.

- *Analysis of Combat Support Basing Options,* Mahyar A. Amouzegar, Lionel A. Galway, and Robert S. Tripp (MG-261-AF). This monograph presents an analytical framework for evaluating alternative FSL options. A central component of this work is an optimization model that allows a user to select the best mix of land-based and sea-based FSLs for a given set of operational scenarios, thereby reducing costs while supporting a range of contingency operations.

RAND Project AIR FORCE

RAND Project AIR FORCE (PAF), a division of the RAND Corporation, is the Air Force's federally funded research and development center for studies and analyses. PAF provides the Air Force with independent analyses of policy alternatives affecting the development, employment, combat readiness, and support of current and future aerospace forces. Research is conducted in four programs: Aerospace

Force Development; Manpower, Personnel, and Training; Resource Management; and Strategy and Doctrine.

Additional information about PAF is available on our Web site at http://www.rand.org/paf.

Contents

CHAPTER THREE

**Tools and Technology Requirements for Sense and Respond
    Combat Support** 37

Figures

Tables

Summary

Sense and respond logistics (S&RL) or, more broadly, sense and respond combat support (S&RCS), has been the subject of much discussion. However, many of its operational components have not been fully envisioned and both current and projected technological apparatus is limited. Moreover, it is not clear how these components can be incorporated or function within a military logistics or combat system. This monograph identifies the elements of S&RCS and shows what is necessary to use the concept within the military, and more specifically the Air Force, combat support system. The monograph further surveys the state of technology necessary to implement S&RCS capabilities within the military and identifies both the technical work that needs to be further developed and the Air Force organization most appropriate to manage the development of these capabilities.

Military S&RCS Defined: Integration of Predictive, Responsiveness, and Command and Control Capabilities

S&RCS capabilities involve predicting what will be needed and responding quickly to anticipated or unanticipated needs to maintain military capabilities. In the past, theories about prediction and responsiveness were framed as *competitive* concepts. This monograph shows the need for both *predictive* tools and *responsive* systems working together within a combat support command and control (CSC2) framework to create military capabilities. Although some elements of S&RCS have been exercised throughout the Air Force's history, years were required to develop and understand the relationship between predictive tools and responsive logistics management and processes and make it feasible to design a responsive and adaptive combat support (CS) system able to meet today's and tomorrow's defense challenges in a more effective and efficient manner. Recently, conceptual, political, budgetary, and technological developments have converged, necessitating and permitting the transformation from traditional logistics support policies and practices into a comprehensive agile combat support (ACS) system able to achieve the required balance among scarce resources and improved processes that can replace mass with speed (i.e., large numbers of assets in place versus rapid distribution of smaller increments of resources as they are needed or consumed). CSC2 is key to this transformation. The Air Force vision of the CSC2 architecture and current implementation actions of that architecture are important steps in overseeing and coordinating the complex set of support functions essential to reliable support of military operations.

It is important to distinguish the inclusive concept of combat support from the smaller subset of logistics. The traditional, but narrower, definition of logistics includes the disciplines of supply, maintenance, transportation, logistics plans, munitions, and sometimes contracting. The smaller subset is commonly referred to as logistics with a little "l". Combat support is sometimes referred to as logistics with a big "L", since it incorporates all aspects of establishing and supporting a base of military operations. Combat support incorporates all of the little "l" logistics areas but also civil engineering, force protection, billeting, messing, and other services required to support a fighting force in the field.

This monograph focuses on the larger view of logistics, which incorporates the broader concept of all CS requirements. Blending principles of S&RL with the broader and inclusive definition of combat support, we have created the acronym S&RCS, which we use throughout this study. S&RCS is an essential piece in combat support that facilitates ACS.

The CSC2 Architecture

One contribution of this monograph is to define the relationship between CSC2 and S&RCS. This monograph presents CSC2 as a key enabler of S&RCS and indicates why it is necessary to implement S&RCS in military applications. CSC2 involves the following:

- Joint development of a plan (campaign, peacetime training, or others) in which logistics process performance and resource levels are related to desired operational effects, e.g., projected weapon system availability, forward operating location initial operating capability, and so forth. The development of a joint plan requires prediction and models to translate logistics process performance and resource levels to operationally relevant measures of effectiveness for the plan. Draft plans are iterated until a feasible plan is generated. These feasibility assessments require models and predictions to determine if assumed logistics process performance and resources allocated to the plan can meet desired operational effects. To support rapid global deployment and employment objectives, the Air Force has geared deployment so that fewer resources are deployed with combat units, requiring less material to be initially deployed and therefore allowing more rapid deployment of the unit. The Air Force then relies on responsive resupply to support ongoing operational activities.
- Establishment of logistics process performance and resource-level control parameters that are necessary to achieve the desired operational objectives.
- Execution of the plan and tracking of control parameters against actual process performance and resource levels to achieve specific operational effects. This is the sense part of the CSC2 system. The system senses when deviations in logistics system performance will affect operational performance. This is critical to military activities. Many subsystems may not be performing as well as they could, and yet their performance may not affect operational

outcomes. The system must be able to differentiate between insignificant degradations in performance and CS shortfalls that will constrain operations.

- Signaling logistics process owners when their processes lie outside control limits. When logistics performance is likely to adversely affect operational outcomes, action is necessary to correct the process performance or to adjust logistics resource levels to conform to the actual process performance, e.g., if transportation is slower than planned, additional resource levels at the deployed location may have to be authorized if transportation cannot be made quicker, as may be the case in high-threat environments. Prediction capabilities are critical here, because the aim of S&RCS capabilities is to identify CS problems *before* they have a negative effect on operational objectives.

- Replan logistics or operational components of the plan to mitigate the portions of the plan that are outside control limits. This affects the plan and new control limits will need to be established and the process of tracking performance continued. This sense and respond (S&R) system then continues indefinitely.

Modern CSC2 capabilities, as well as future improvements, can be used by the Department of Defense (DoD) and the Air Force to build an efficient system of S&RCS in and among the military services. More significantly, today's emerging CSC2 capabilities are facilitating the move to S&RCS. In the past, limits in CSC2 have prevented a robust and systematic S&RCS capability. Today, a convergence of CS doctrine and capability makes S&RCS possible. These new capabilities will allow the Air Force to translate operational requirements into logistical requirements, set control parameters, sense, and respond to out-of-control conditions. In short, the Air Force can achieve S&RCS capabilities in the challenging military environment if it continues along the path of upgrading the CSC2 architecture, information systems, organizations, and training of CS personnel. (See pp. 20–27.)

Technology Necessary to Create S&CS Capabilities

The DoD Office of Force Transformation (OFT) developed the military sense and respond logistics concept, borrowing heavily from research in the commercial sector (which was in turn indebted to earlier military efforts) to describe an adaptive method for maintaining operational availability of units by managing their end-to-end support network.[1] OFT identified a number of technologies that are needed to produce an S&RL capability, two of which were highlighted as especially important components: radio frequency identification (RFID) and intelligent (adaptive) software agents. RFID is an Automatic Identification Technology (AIT) that provides location and status information for items in the CS system. RFID technologies are fairly mature and have been fielded in both commercial and military arenas.

Agent-based modeling allows a more robust simulation of combat support operations. Agent-based models (ABMs) have been used extensively in combat modeling but, until very recently, there has been limited application in the logistics area. A number of initiatives developed by the Defense Advanced Research Project Agency have examined the use of ABMs in the CS domain; however, these technologies are still in their early stages.

This monograph summarizes a number of key DoD and commercial initiatives to implement S&RL technologies and identifies a promising DoD trial (OFT's S&RL Information Technology prototype) along with one successfully fielded commercial system (developed by General Electric Transportation Systems). However, an important conclusion of this review is that although current technology has enabled a limited set of sense and respond capabilities, a full implementation of S&RL concepts remains dependent on substantial future technological development. The largest challenge ahead for implementing a broader S&RCS capability is the development of an understanding of the interactions between combat support system performance and combat operational metrics. (See p. 37.)

---

[1] U.S. DoD (2003).

An Implementation Path for Creating Air Force S&RCS Capabilities

The Air Force has already begun to take steps to implement some of these concepts and technologies with varying degrees of success. Air Force implementation actions include making doctrine changes to recognize the importance of CSC2, as part of S&RCS capabilities, and identifying training and information system improvements.

In addition, the Air Force should identify one organization to lead development of CSC2 and associated S&RCS capabilities. This would facilitate the development of these capabilities. Currently, the Air Force Command and Control Intelligence, Surveillance, and Reconnaissance Center (AFC2ISRC) is tasked with developing and testing C2 tools. The AFC2ISRC has an A4 (logistics) staff element that could exercise responsibility for developing and leveraging existing CSC2 and S&RCS tools under the AFC2ISRC charter. This lead role would need to be supported by the AFC2ISRC/CC and A4/7 (formerly AF/IL) and the AFC2ISRC mission statement might need to be revised to emphasize the importance of the CSC2 and S&RCS development responsibility. Staffing levels to accomplish the new responsibilities may need to be reviewed to ensure that they are adequate to handle the added responsibilities. (See pp. 71–72.)

Acknowledgments

This monograph outlines the development of military sense and respond combat support concepts, especially those developed within the U.S. Air Force. Over the years, several people in the Air Force have supported the development of the concepts explained here. Many of them are acknowledged in the research cited in this monograph. The senior leaders who sponsored work in this area were people of vision who had the patience to invest research capital in a difficult and complex field and to wait years for payback. Many in the Air Force helped gather data, support visits to operational and support locations, and test the concepts before implementation of the concepts took place.

This report was sponsored by Grover Dunn, A4I (formerly AF/ILI), Director of Innovation and Transformation. He provided the guidance to closely link this effort to ongoing Air Force transformation efforts. Colonels Chris O'Hara, A4RX (formerly AF/ILGX), and Paul Dunbar, A4I (formerly AF/ILI), have also been instrumental in keeping this study closely aligned with their work with modernized information enterprise modernization.

Many RAND researchers also contributed to this field of study and the concepts discussed in this monograph. They include Bernice Brown and her colleagues in the 1950s who indicated that logistics processes in the Air Force dealt with problems of uncertainty and, therefore, prediction of precise logistics parameters may never be possible. They indicated that hedging strategies and responsive management adaptations could effect changes in logistics process performance and thereby mitigate problems associated with poor forecasting capabilities.

Throughout the 1970s, 1980s, and 1990s, Craig Sherbrooke, Richard Hillestad, Manuel Carrillo, Louis Miller, Jack Abell, and others developed models that related how individual items and processes could affect weapon system availability. Their models have become embedded in inventory computation, depot-level maintenance workloading, and capability assessment methods.

Gordon Crawford pointed out again in the 1980s that uncertainty and difficulties in forecasting spare parts demands still existed.

Irv Cohen, Jack Abell, and Tom Lippiatt developed the notion that logistics and operations had to be closely linked to respond to uncertainties and potential enemy actions. Ray Pyles, Tim Ramey, Hyman Shulman, and Irv Cohen developed thoughts on "lean logistics" and how responsive logistics processes could better support dynamic warfighter needs, often more efficiently than the "just-in-case" support system.

Hyman Shulman and others indicated that the product line that the logistics system was designed to support was a fully capable weapon system including fuel and munitions. They also predicted that resource shortages of one form or another were inevitable. If these assertions are correct, then a command and control system is needed to allocate scarce resources to weapon systems most in need. This system must therefore predict resource needs and be able to allocate scarce resources to where they are needed most—across many different time horizons. Thus, Air Force inventory, maintenance, procurement, and other logistics systems must be able to forecast resource needs for any given plan, to assess the effects of shortages on operational performance, and then to help orchestrate these systems' outputs to achieve whatever operational goals were needed and funded.

We also benefited greatly during our project by contributions from Margaret Blume-Kohout, Tom Lang, and Louis Luangkesorn. Finally, We would like to thank Fran Teague for her assistance in handling the many revisions of this monograph.

The bibliography contains a more complete list of those who have contributed to this body of research.

Abbreviations

A4/7 (formerly AF/IL	Air Force Deputy Chief of Staff for Installations and Logistics
ABLE	Agent Building and Learning Environment
ABM	agent-based model
ACC	Air Combat Command
ACES	Agile Combat Execution Support
ACS	agile combat support
AEF	Air and Space Expeditionary Force
AFC2ISRC	Air Force Command and Control, Intelligence, Surveillance, and Reconnaissance Center
AFIT	Air Force Institute of Technology
AFFOR	Air Force Forces
AFI	Air Force Instruction
AFMC	Air Force Materiel Command
AFRL	Air Force Research Laboratories
AGE	Aerospace Ground Equipment
AIT	automatic identification technology
AL	autonomic logistics
ALC	Air Logistics Center
ALP	Advanced Logistics Project
AMC	Air Mobility Command
AOC	Air Operations Center
AOR	area of responsibility
APS	advanced planning and scheduling
ART	AEF UTC reporting tool

AT&L	Acquisition, Technology, and Logistics
ATP	available-to-promise
AWOS	Air War Over Serbia
BEAR	Basic Expeditionary Airfield Resources
BES	Budget Estimate Submission
C2	command and control
C4	command, control, communications, and computers
C4ISR	command, control, communications, computers, intelligence, surveillance, and reconnaissance
CAF	Combat Air Forces
CAP	Crisis Action Planning
CCP	commodity control point
CENTAF	Central Air Forces
CIRF	centralized intermediate repair facility
COA	course of action
CoAX	Coalition Agent eXperiment
COMAFFOR	Commander of the Air Force Air Forces
CONOP	concept of operation
CONUS	continental United States
COTS	commercial off-the-shelf
CS	combat support
CSC	combat support center
CSC2	combat support command and control
CSCW	computer support and cooperative work
CSE	combat support element
CSL	CONUS support location
DAO	Distributed Adaptive Operations
DARPA	Defense Advanced Research Projects Agency
DCTS	Defense Collaboration Tool Suite
DoD	Department of Defense
DPG	Defense Planning Guidance
DR	disaster relief
DRC	Dynamic Resource Corporation

EAF	Expeditionary Aerospace Force
ECM	electronic countermeasures
EPM	EXPRESS Planning Module
ERP	enterprise resource planning
EUCOM	European Command
EXPRESS	Execution and Prioritization of Repair Support System
FLE	Force-Centric Logistics Enterprise
FLOW	Focused Logistics Wargame
FMSE	fuel mobility support equipment
FOL	forward operating location
FSL	forward support location
FYDP	Future Years Defense Program
GCCS	Global Combat Support System
GPS	global positioning system
HA	humanitarian assistance
IEDA	Integrated Enterprise Domain Architecture
IOC	initial operational capability
IT	information technology
ITV	In-Transit Visibility
JAOC	Joint Air Operations Center
JCN	job control number
JEIM	Jet Engine Intermediate Maintenance
JFACC	Joint Forces Air Component Commander
JFCOM	Joint Forces Command
JSF	Joint Strike Fighter
JTF	Joint Task Force
LANTIRN	Low Altitude Navigation and Targeting Infrared for Night
LRU	line replaceable unit
LSA	Logistics Supportability Analysis
LSC	logistics support center
LTA	Logistics Transformation Agency
MAF	Mobility Air Forces

MAJCOM	Major Command
MALT	Multi-Agent Logistics Tool
MANA	Map Aware Non-Uniform Automata
MDS	Mission Design Series
MOE	measure of effectiveness
MOG	maximum on ground
NAF	Numbered Air Force
NCOW	Network-Centric Operations and Warfare
NCW	Network-Centric Warfare
OAF	Operation Allied Force
OEF	Operation Enduring Freedom
OFT	Office of Force Transformation
OIF	Operation Iraqi Freedom
OODA	observe, orient, decide, and act
OPT	operational parameters template
OPTEMPO	operational tempo
OS	operating system
OSC	Operations Support Center
OSD	Office of the Secretary of Defense
PACAF	Pacific Air Forces
PACOM	Pacific Command
PAF	Project AIR FORCE
PPBE	planning, programming, budgeting, and execution
POL	petroleum, oils, and lubricants
POM	Program Objective Memorandum
POSC	PACAF OSC
PSA	Predictive Support Awareness
RETSINA	Reusable Environment for Task-Structured Intelligent Networked Agents
RFID	radio frequency identification
RN	requisition number
RSS	Regional Supply Squadron
S&RCS	sense and respond combat support
S&RL	sense and respond logistics

SAR	sense and respond
SCM	Supply Chain Management
SCN	Supply Chain Network
SIDA	sense, interpret, decide, act
SOS	source of supply
TCN	transportation control number
TDS	Theater Distribution System
TPFDD	Time-Phased Force Deployment Data
USAFE	U.S. Air Forces Europe
USMC	U.S. Marine Corps
USTRANSCOM	U.S. Transportation Command
UTASC	USAFE Theater Air Support Center
UTC	unit type code
WRM	War Reserve Materiel
XML	Extensible Markup Language

CHAPTER ONE

Introduction

The inefficiencies of the military logistical system in the early 20th century spurred a modern scientific study of logistics. Most of the early supply system operated on a "push" concept rather than in response to actual needs and changes. It was thought that having an abundance of resources in theater ensured that combat support (CS) elements would be able to provide everything needed to achieve the desired operational effects. In practice, the presence of "mountains of supplies" did not always ensure that warfighters' demands were met. In fact, the backlog of war materiel congested the CS system because of inefficiencies in the transportation system and the prioritization processes. It was evident that a more comprehensive capability was needed for matching CS assets to warfighter needs. In the past, prediction and responsiveness have been viewed as competing concepts; we show that both are necessary and can be integrated within a command and control system to create military sense and respond capabilities.

Military logistics planning grew even more difficult with the collapse of the Soviet Union and the dissolution of the associated threat to U.S. interests in Europe. For although the previous CS system was inefficient in its use of resources, it was at least focused on (presumably) known geographic locations and specific threats. The geopolitical divide that once defined U.S. military policy was replaced by a temporary rise of regional hegemons; the geopolitical environment, in turn, slowly evolved (and continues to evolve) into one that is defined not only by regional powers but also by nontraditional security threats. The uncertainty associated with planning for military operations was thus extended to include uncertainty about the *locations* and *purpose* of operations.

The Air and Space Expeditionary Force Construct

The Air and Space Expeditionary Force (AEF)[1] concept is a transformational construct that changed the Air Force's mindset from a threat-based, forward-deployed force designed to fight the Cold War to a primarily continental United States (CONUS)–positioned, rotational, and effects-based force able to respond rapidly to a variety of threats while accommodating a high operational tempo (OPTEMPO) in the face of the uncertainties inherent in today's contingency environment. The AEF is intended to be able to deploy small or large force and support packages anywhere in the world and put bombs on target in very short time frames—in as little as 72 hours at some sites. The transformational objective of the AEF is a reliance on rapid response rather than on forward presence. The new concept was intended to lead to greater flexibility and a smaller CS footprint and, at the same time, reduced personnel turnover.

An Expeditionary Force Requires Agile Combat Support

The fielding of the AEF prompted a fundamental rethinking and restructuring of logistics. Traditionally, logistics has included maintenance, supply, and transportation, referred to as logistics with a little "l." The modern perspective of CS, also referred to as logistics with a big "L," recognizes that CS must incorporate all the traditional logistics areas as well as civil engineering; services (billeting and messing); force protection; basing; and command, control, communications, and

---

[1]   Early in its development, the term Expeditionary Aerospace Force (EAF) was used to describe the concept of employing Air Force forces rapidly anywhere in the world in pre-defined force packages called Aerospace Expeditionary Forces. The terms have since evolved and the Air Force now uses the term Air and Space Expeditionary Force to describe both the concept and force packages.

computers (C4). This is the CS concept that will be discussed throughout this report. It is important to recognize that all these CS elements are interrelated. Each is critical in the total CS view and any one element can limit or control the performance of the others.

The shift to a more expeditionary force compelled a movement within the Air Force toward a capability called agile combat support (ACS). The definition of ACS began to emerge as described in a series of Air Force and RAND publications,[2] detailing both micro- and macro-level analyses. The results of several years of analysis by RAND and the Air Force called for a new CS infrastructure consisting of forward operating locations (FOLs), forward support locations (FSLs), CONUS support locations (CSLs), a well-orchestrated worldwide distribution system, and a robust and responsive combat support command and control (CSC2) architecture. Forward positioning of heavy logistics commodities, such as munitions, fuel, and intermediate maintenance assets, was identified as a prerequisite to the realization of the AEF's rapid force deployment objectives. Furthermore, because no combatant commander possessed all of the logistics resources needed to initiate and sustain combat operations, an emphasis was placed on capabilities to rapidly distribute (deploy and sustain) resources, from where they were stored or available to where they would be employed, and to control the distribution of scarce resources to the units that needed them most. These actions constitute the components of a modern CSC2—assessing needs and determining what is required in operationally relevant terms. The Air Force has realized the importance of CSC2 architecture and has begun to implement many of these ACS concepts as a key enabler to the AEF.

Table 1.1 outlines the important ACS capabilities that help to achieve desired operational effects. The Air Force stressed the concepts of light, lean, and lethal and began to look at ways to establish "lean" pipelines through both improved planning (predicting and

---

[2] See Tripp, Galway, Killingsworth, et al. (1999); Tripp, Galway, Ramey, et al. (2000); Galway et al. (2000); Peltz et al. (2000); Amouzegar, Galway, and Geller (2002); Amouzegar, Galway, and Tripp (2004); Amouzegar, Tripp, McGarvey, et al. (2004); and Rainey et al. (2003).

Table 1.1
Operational Effects and ACS Capabilities

Desired Operational Effect	ACS Capability/Action to Enable Effect
Foster an expeditionary mindset	Develop CS leaders who understand expeditionary operations
	Instill expeditionary mindset in CS personnel
	Develop expeditionary scheduling rules
Configure support rapidly	Establish robust CSC2 capabilities
	Estimate resource needs quickly
	Tailor ACS network to scenario rapidly
	Establish ACS control parameters for feasible plans
	Track performance against control parameters
	Modify processes as necessary
	Establish robust end-to-end distribution capabilities
Deploy/employ quickly	Rapid FOL site survey techniques
	Robust FOL development capability
	Attention to engagement policies and pre-surveys
	Lean deployment packages and reduced deployed footprint
	Rapid deployment of non-unit resources (War Reserve Materiel [WRM])
Shift to sustainment smoothly	Enhanced FSL/CSL linkages to resupply FOLs
Maintain readiness for scenarios outlined in DoD strategic planning guidance	Align resource planning factors to reflect current rotational and contingency employment practices
Reduce CS footprint	Exploit technology—communications, munitions, etc.

forecasting) and more responsive policies and processes to shorten resupply pipelines and to compensate for the inability to accurately predict some support requirements. The move toward more lean logistics was necessary to meet the new mission requirements at multiple fixed and deployed locations with fewer resources. Air Force logistics planners realized that the imprecision of these predictions, along with the increased uncertainty in the geopolitical environment, place a premium on CS that is flexible, adaptable, and responsive. Most important, these planners recognized the need to establish linkages between CS and *operational effects*.

The ability of CS forces to sense the operational environment accurately, and then adapt swiftly to develop tailored responses to the operational requirements, is essential to achieving warfighters' objectives and effects effectively and efficiently. This is not a new observation and was applicable to the old security environment. As early as 1977, the concept of the observe, orient, decide, and act (OODA) loop was used to guide combat planning and analysis at the tactical level.[3] In the CS enterprise, sensing and adapting quickly ensures an uninterrupted flow of critical CS materiel to the warfighter, arriving when and where it is needed. Deployed assets and supporting materiel need to be tailored to achieve specific, quantifiable operational effects. Deploying mountains of just-in-case support equipment and supplies has ceased to be part of modern CS strategy. However, a purely *reactive* system that intervenes only *after* logistics problems inhibit the operational plans does not benefit the warfighter. What is needed is a *proactive* system that can *monitor* logistics system performance, *analyze* current system data to predict future constraints (both near term and long term) that the CS system will place on operational objectives, and *identify mitigations* to minimize the effect of these constraints.

Military logisticians of the past were able to overcome the lack of such a "sense and respond" capability partly because of their in-

---

[3] Alberts et al. (2001). Warfighters have reiterated similar concepts throughout modern warfare, as is clear from Air Marshall Giulio Douhet's 1928 statement: "Victory smiles upon those who anticipate the changes in the character of war, not upon those who wait to adapt themselves after the changes occur."

position CS and transportation infrastructure, designed around a known geographic location. In the current environment, increased ambiguity has diminished this advantage and increased the need for a sense and respond combat support (S&RCS) capability. CSC2 and responsive processes compose the twin pillars of this S&RCS transformation.

CSC2: An Important Part of ACS and Enabler of S&RCS

Command and control (C2), although often associated with operations (e.g., deploying ships, tasking sorties, battlefield movements), is also a fundamental requirement for effective ACS. As warfighting forces become more flexible in operational tasking, the support system must adapt to become equally flexible. The C2 of modern CS assets must be woven thoroughly with operational events, from planning, through deployment, employment, retasking, and recuperation. Additionally, CS goals and objectives must be increasingly linked directly to operational goals and objectives. The traditional distinction between *operations* and *combat support* loses relevance in such an environment. Combat support activities need to be linked to operational tasking with metrics that have relevance to both warfighter and logistician.

Combat support command and control is the "central processing unit" of a CS system that coordinates and controls the ACS enterprise. In essence, CSC2 sets a framework for the transformation of traditional logistics support into an ACS capability. CSC2 should provide the capabilities to

- Develop plans that take operational scenarios and requirements and couple them with the CS process performance and resource levels allocated to the plan execution to project operational capabilities. This translation of CS performance into operational capabilities requires modeling technology and prediction of CS performance.

- Establish control parameters for the CS process performance and resource levels that are needed to achieve the required operational capabilities.
- Determine a feasible plan that incorporates CS and operational realities.
- Execute the plan and track performance against calculated control parameters.
- Signal all appropriate echelons and process owners when performance parameters are out of control.
- Facilitate the development of operational or CS get-well plans to get the processes back in control or develop new ones, given the realities of current performances.

CSC2 is not simply an information system; rather, it sits on top of functional logistics systems and uses information from them to translate CS process performance and resource levels into operational performance metrics. It also uses information from logistics information systems to track the parameters necessary to control performance. It includes the battlespace management process of planning, directing, coordinating, and controlling forces and operations. Command and control involves the integration of the systems, procedures, organizational structures, personnel, equipment, facilities, information, and communications that enable a commander to exercise C2 across the range of military operations.[4] Previous studies built on this definition of C2 to define CS execution, planning, and control to include the functions of planning, directing, coordinating, and controlling CS resources to meet operational objectives.[5] The objective of this transformed CSC2 architecture is to integrate operational and CS planning in a closed-loop environment, providing feedback on performance and resources.

The new CSC2 components significantly improve planning and control processes, including

---

[4] U.S. Air Force (1997b).

[5] Leftwich et al. (2002).

- ·Planning and forecasting (prediction)
  - joint analysis and planning of CS and operations
  - determining feasibility, establishing control parameters
- Controlling
  - monitoring planned versus actual execution—a feedback loop process allowing for tracking, correction, and replanning when parameters are out of control
- Responsiveness
  - quick pipelines and the ability to respond quickly to change

This comprehensive transformation of CSC2 doctrine and capabilities blends the benefits of continuously updated analytical prediction with the ongoing monitoring of CS systems, which, given a robust transportation capability, enable the rapid response necessary to produce an S&RCS model appropriate for military operations in the 21st century.

The Air Force's initial response to the AEF construct was to define its mission as Global Power–Global Reach with an emphasis on force projection and mobility. *Air Force Vision 2020* further refined the transformational goals and core competencies required to attain these combat capabilities.[6] Although these have been fundamental *conceptual* changes to CS practice, much work remains to match day-to-day reality with the modern concepts.

A New Vision

In parallel with Air Force development of the AEF, the Department of Defense (DoD) responded to the new challenges of the 21st century with a strategic guidance that altered the way the services prepare for conflict. *Joint Vision 2020* described the interoperability that would be required to respond to both current emerging challenges as well as to unknown future possibilities.[7]

---

[6]   U.S. Air Force (2000b).

[7]   U.S. Department of Defense (2000).

The DoD Office of Force Transformation (OFT) was organized and tasked to further define and shape the kind of CS organizations and information systems that would be required to support the concept of Network-Centric Warfare (NCW). The OFT developed a concept based on an adaptive method for maintaining operational availability of units by managing their end-to-end support network.[8] OFT called this concept *military sense and respond logistics*, of which some prominent characteristics include[9]

- a functionally organized network of units (as opposed to a hierarchical organization)
- a realization that all units within the network are potential consumers and providers of supply to and from all other units in the network
- units that dynamically synchronize to satisfy demand in response to changes in the environment.

Sense and respond logistics (S&RL) is a conceptual transformation of logistics systems designed to support the NCW of the future. S&RL emphasizes prediction, anticipation, coordination, and responsive actions and is defined, in program documents, as a key building block in the transformation to an ACS.

The term "S&RL" is derived from the commercial sector; the concept recognizes that *traditional* planning is ineffective in the face of great uncertainty, especially when uncertainty becomes endemic, because contingency plans and situational problem-solving will never be adequate to deal with the steady stream of surprises.[10] The increasing pace of operations and the effects of unpredictable events will at some point overwhelm the means of current planning and execution

---

[8]   U.S. DoD (2003).

[9]   The term "make-and-sell" versus "sense-and-respond" is attributed to Richard Nolan and Stephan Haeckel and their work at IBM. However, the concept of adaptive planning and response, which is at the core of this concept, can be dated back to the OODA loop and other adaptive systems.

[10]   Haeckel (1999).

systems. The commercial sector has come to realize that there is a need for both a strong prediction capability and a capacity to rapidly adapt and react to change. Although this insight is important to modern commercial practice, it is essential when considering the challenges facing today's military operational planners and logisticians.

Defining Sense and Respond Combat Support

The OFT S&RL concept is similar in many respects to the concepts developed during the Air Force study of ACS. The emphasis on the ability to "respond" quickly and appropriately through the C2 function to the broader areas constituting CS is how we differentiate S&RCS from S&RL. Implementing S&RL concepts and technologies through the CSC2 architecture is the way to achieve an S&RCS capability.

In commercial S&RL and a volatile market, the manufacturer and distributor constantly monitor changes in buying patterns and adapt quickly to maintain market share. By employing S&RL, commercial enterprise has been able to reduce investments in warehouses and stock. Industry now increasingly produces what is desired and required rather than what a planner thinks should be built based on internal production goals. Commercial S&RL, in theory, reduces stock and overhead costs and responds rapidly to change.[11] The key to these improvements is a robust system of information-gathering and analysis or, in military terms, a highly efficient C2 system.

We have determined that commercial practices and commercial definitions of S&RL fall short of what is needed to create S&RCS in the Air Force environment. Although there are similarities between some of the issues and constraints of the military and those of a large corporation, the risk of human casualty, the consequences to the international political order, and vastly different military objectives set the DoD apart from any corporation of comparable size. The scope of activities included in military CS is also much broader than that of

---

[11] Military readers should equate the word customer, in civilian literature, to operational effects.

commercial logistics; any reorganizational concept must consider the nuances of military operations. It is interesting to note that firms have designed lean supply chains to be resilient to business disruptions,[12] but it has been shown that resiliency for firms may not translate to resiliency for the entire supply chain and government provision of pliability and redundancy may be necessary in an era of lean supply chain management.[13] In the military case, the Air Force is the sole user and provider and thus the business notions of resiliency may not be entirely applicable.

Sense and respond combat support, as in commercial S&RL, attempts to strike a balance between a purely responsive system and a purely predictive one. Consider an example of munitions storage, handling, and delivery. At the strategic level, the emphasis is on the location and allocation of munitions prepositioning, based on an assessment of future needs. At the tactical and execution levels, for a given network of munitions storage locations and transportation links, the emphasis is shifted to a more adaptive supply chain with an integrated C2, wherein units attempt to sense demand, consider delivery and production capabilities, and respond with timely supply of the warfighter's requirements. The resolution of sense and respond (S&R) is continually in flux and depends on the intensity of the OPTEMPO. Although forecasting models are continually improved, many factors cannot be modeled with the desired accuracy. For this reason, actual performance must be constantly measured against planned performance. When discrepancies are identified, adjustments are made to the plans at *all* levels (strategic, tactical, and execution), as needed. This is achieved through perpetually employed sensors, a feedback loop in the C2 system, and an adaptive response system, all working in unison.

This example demonstrates the need for CS processes to be more thoroughly embedded in every step of operational planning and execution, which will present a new opportunity for cooperation between CS and operations personnel. Traditionally, ongoing planning and tasking often occur in isolation from those who would subsequently be

---

[12] Sheffi (2005).

[13] See for example Willis and Ortiz (2004).

required to support the levels and rates of tasking. Coordination, if any, occurs after initial planning cycles are completed. Modern, responsive systems demand information-sharing among all partners in the military enterprise.

Combat support disconnects from operations are not the only ones that degrade sensing capability. Legacy systems, within logistics functional areas, are also not fully integrated. Data and information are captured in stove-piped systems that meet the information needs of only a narrow community. The Air Force's CS legacy systems are good examples of enterprises that have no provision for cross-flow of information, not only *between* supply, transportation, and maintenance but often not even *within* the family of other supply, maintenance, or transportation data systems.

These stove-piped systems are not unique to the military. The deleterious effects of stove-piped systems in commercial practice are evidenced by a multitude of independent commercial networks that are incompatible technically, contributing to the inhibition of information-sharing. Consequently, disjointed decisionmaking occurs—one of the largest impediments to realizing technology's potential contributions to the management of large companies.[14]

A Military Idea Turned Commercial

As mentioned above, some of the fundamental concepts employed in the commercial practice of S&RL had their origins in military (especially Air Force) lessons learned. Ideas originally elucidated by Colonel John Boyd, based on his Korean War experience as a fighter pilot, were subsequently reshaped and applied, first by Stephan Haeckel, then by other business analysts and practitioners.[15]

In his attempt to explain the wartime combat successes of U.S. fighter pilots over their North Korean counterparts, Boyd deduced a concept that he called the observe, orient, decide, and act (OODA)

---

[14] Haeckel (1996).

[15] Menotti (2004).

loop. The OODA loop essentially states that if one makes informed decisions and takes action faster than one's enemy, then one will outperform the enemy. As the speed of this OODA loop cycle increases, the enemy continually remains, both tactically and intellectually, a step behind. Boyd's work was followed by other research that focused on proactive response within closed-loop information systems.[16]

The commercial sense, interpret, decide, act (SIDA) loop is an adaptation of Boyd's original concept. The business community observed the effect of the OODA loop in the military and recognized its applicability toward achieving a more flexible and responsive business design. In effect, Haeckel "civilianized" the OODA loop cycle and applied it to business, radically reshaping modern corporate thinking. Boyd's ideas, applied in the commercial world, have helped companies systematically cope with the unexpected. Nomenclature aside, the main argument remains the same: When the effects of unpredictability cannot be mitigated, an adaptive strategy is required—sensing early and responding quickly to abrupt changes in customer needs.

Ultimately, the military and commercial programs matured in parallel, with successes in one arena affecting the other. However, in the current environment, the Air Force (and all DoD) must develop an even greater S&R capability, beyond what has been achieved in commercial practice. We believe that the required S&RCS capability can best be realized through the implementation of S&RL technologies (both existing and those yet to be developed) into the CSC2 architecture. The path toward such an S&RCS is the focus of this monograph.

Organization of This Monograph

Chapter Two explains the various components of CSC2 and the CSC2 operational architecture that guides development of the system. It

---

[16] This category of information analysis and response in a closed system is called cybernetics. Research in this area also preceded Haeckel's writings. See, for instance, Tripp and Rainey (1985).

explains how each component fits with the others, and its relationship to functional CS systems and the Air Force enterprise architecture. It examines the necessary linkages between the business information systems and the data from them, which must be passed to the combat C2 systems to effect appropriate responses to out-of-control conditions.

Chapter Three describes current and emerging technologies, which will assist the CSC2 requirements for processed, actionable information to be assembled using current and modernized business process information systems in support of S&RCS development.

Chapter Four relates the progress that the Air Force has made to grow this new CSC2 architecture into a fully operable concept and system. It includes a discussion of the information renewal efforts under way to modernize business processes and their associated information systems. It also explains the emerging relationship between the CSC2 operational architecture and systems and the CS operational architecture and systems.

The last chapter explains what remains to be done: Significant pieces of the CSC2 architecture still require enhancement, even creation. The S&RL technologies will need to be integrated into this architecture in a strategic fashion to ultimately enable an S&RCS capability for the Air Force.

The Air Force has made strides toward a more responsive, more effective CS system. A critical component of the new S&RCS, or ACS, is CSC2. This monograph highlights the successes of the past, while pointing the way to actions to complete the transformation necessary to create an effective CSC2 with S&RCS capabilities as a component of ACS.

CHAPTER TWO

The CSC2 Operational Architecture

This chapter presents the highlights of the CSC2 operational architecture that is a critical part of both the AEF transformational concept and S&RCS capabilities, focusing on the key organizations that participate in the planning, budgeting, and executing of CS activities.[1]

A CSC2 system oversees the performance of CS processes and resource levels to ensure that they are within the specified levels needed to achieve specific CS effects, such as FOL initial operational capability (IOC), or F-15 sortie-generation capability.[2] The CSC2 system monitors CS parameters (e.g., maintenance and transport times) against the target values necessary to achieve desired CS effects in a given contingency operation or training scenario. The system "signals" the appropriate C2 nodes and process owners when process performance parameters violate certain thresholds. Such a CSC2 *system* would enable an S&RCS *capability*, with the ultimate goal of linking CS performance to operational effects.

Previous research has developed a CSC2 operational architecture that provides one view of such a system.[3] This chapter presents these high-level TO-BE processes, along with the various CSC2 nodes and

---

[1] For a more detailed examination of AS-IS and TO-BE CSC2 operational architecture concepts, see Leftwich et al. (2002); and Mills et al. (2004).

[2] Ultimately, the CSC2 system should relate how CS performance and resource levels affect operational effects, but current theoretical understanding limits the relationships to CS effects.

[3] Leftwich et al. (2002); and Mills et al. (2006).

their activities and procedures. The CSC2 architecture specifies the need for the following support:

- standing CS organizations
- planning, programming, and execution that relates operational effects to CS resource requirements
- capability assessment and reporting
- information security
- programming and budgeting linked to shortfalls.

This chapter discusses the relationship between CSC2 and the planning, programming, budgeting, and execution (PPBE) system to emphasize that S&RCS capabilities are needed across *both* strategic and execution time horizons.

The USAFE Centralized Intermediate Repair Facility— A Recent Example

As the U.S. Air Force transitioned from a garrison-based force to an AEF, logisticians were tasked to develop ACS concepts that enhanced warfighting capability. During Operation Allied Force (OAF), the Air Force successfully demonstrated the concept of the centralized intermediate repair facility (CIRF), which leveraged existing intermediate repair facilities in the European Command (EUCOM) theater of operations to meet mission requirements. The CIRF in U.S. Air Forces Europe (USAFE)—a wing-level facility—was expanded to provide repair support for multiple Air Force units within the same theater of operations. The CIRF methodology replaced the traditional decentralized repair maintenance concept in which wing-level units perform all intermediate-level maintenance (ILM) for both home-stationed and deployed aircraft. At the end of OAF combat operations, USAFE was tasked to test this concept more fully and to gather data that would help to evaluate the relative merits of CIRF operations. The test analyzed data accumulated while supporting actual AEF rotations.[4] In this test, two CIRFs (at Royal Air Force Lakenheath, United Kingdom, and Spangdahlem Air Base, Germany) supported the units and equipment for Electronic Warfare and Low Altitude Navigation and Targeting Infrared for Night (LANTIRN) pods, two engine types, and avionics line replaceable units (LRUs) for one Mission Design Series (MDS).

Figure 2.1 depicts the S&RCS capability associated with this CIRF example, using a closed-loop planning, assessment, and control framework. In this example, F-15 sortie generation capability is a function of many variables including

- removal rates and LRU levels at the FOLs
- maintenance actions taken at the CIRF, and distribution throughput in and outside the theater
- transportation timelines, both to and from the CIRF
- surge capability
- aircraft availability.

Given the above sensor points, Air Force logisticians need to ensure that CS process performance supports the F-15 planned sortie generation capability. If it is unable to do so, trigger systems need to alert CS personnel to the options available for recommendation to the appropriate command levels.

We will return to this example throughout this chapter as components of the CSC2 operational architecture are introduced.

High-Level CSC2 Processes

A robust CSC2 construct will enable an S&RCS capability that integrates operational and CS planning in a closed-loop environment, providing feedback on performance and resources. Figure 2.2 illustrates this concept in a process template that can be applied through all phases of an operation from readiness, planning, deployment,

---

[4] See Geller et al. (2004).

Figure 2.1
Combat Support Performance Parameters Are Related to Operational Measures of Effectiveness

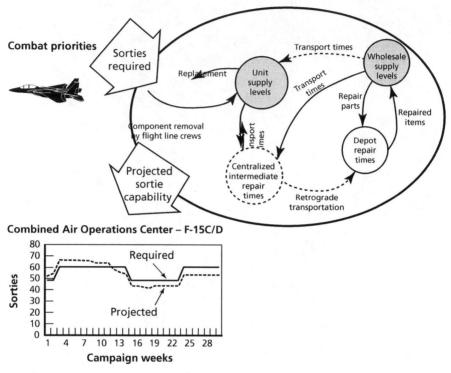

employment, and sustainment to redeployment and reconstitution. The figure centers on integrated operations/CS planning and incorporates activities for continually monitoring and adjusting performance. Some elements of the process, shaded in medium gray in Figure 2.2, take place in planning for operations and should be accomplished with operational planners.

Feedback Loops

A key element of both planning and execution in this process template is the feedback loop that specifies how well the system is expected to perform (during planning) and contrasts these expectations with observations of the system performance realized during execution. If

Figure 2.2
Feedback Loop Process

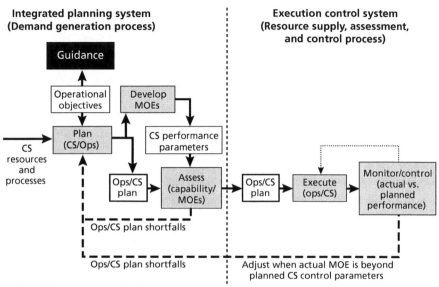

NOTE: MOE = measure of effectiveness.

actual performance deviates significantly from planned performance, the CSC2 system warns the appropriate CS processes that their performance may jeopardize operational objectives. This CSC2 system must be able to differentiate small discrepancies that do not warrant C2 notification from substantial ones that might compromise future operations. This requires the identification of *tolerance limits* for all parameters, which is heavily dependent on improved prediction capabilities. This feedback loop process identifies when the CS plan and infrastructure need to be reconfigured to meet dynamic operational requirements and notifies the logistics and installations support planners to take action, during both planning and execution. The CS organizations need to be responsive and adaptive to make timely changes in execution. The process not only drives changes in the CS plan but may also call for a shift in the operational plan. For the CS system to provide timely feedback to operators, it must be tightly coupled to their planning and execution processes and systems, providing options that explain the interrelationships between effects and costs. Feedback might include notification of missions that cannot be performed because of CS limitations.

In the CIRF example, if there are indications that CIRF transport times may exceed those necessary to meet specific weapon system performance goals, the process owners need to develop plans to correct this performance and notify the appropriate C2 node of the proposed solution and costs. The C2 node would approve suggested get-well plans and request resources to correct the process. Transport personnel would try to change transport service capabilities to bring the system back within control limits for transport times. If transport capability cannot be corrected because of supply constraints, the C2 node would facilitate dialog with maintenance personnel to change the maintenance concept for the affected bases where transport times were outside control limits. This may require the deployment of maintenance capabilities to FOLs that were being supported by the CIRF. If the deployment of maintenance is too costly, stock levels need to be supplemented to offset slower transport times. Again, the C2 node decides, with inputs from operational and CS commands, which solution to pursue.

In this example, it can be seen that the ultimate goal is to achieve operational objectives by maintaining established readiness levels. The effects of maintenance, transportation, and supply solutions are interrelated. Several solutions may be possible to effect change in levels of weapon system readiness. The prerequisite for choosing among the possible get-well actions is a robust data system with critical pieces of logistics information. Information extracted from these systems must be appropriate, timely, accurate, and automatically refreshed.

Continuous Monitoring of Important Parameters
The CSC2 system should continuously monitor combat support performance and resource levels against the changes in the parameters required by the get-well solution. This continuous, closed-loop process and resource level monitoring is a critical part of the CSC2 system facilitating S&RCS. However, a true S&RCS capability should not simply act as a thermostat. That is, it should not be merely reactive— only checking to see if a certain parameter has breached a threshold before eliciting a response. In a sense, a fully functioning S&RCS

system should act more like a weather forecasting gauge, constantly checking not only the performance of a single parameter but all pertinent parameters simultaneously (e.g., not just temperature but air pressure and wind patterns as well) for comparison against their target values. In both S&RCS and the weather forecasting systems, the goal is an early notification of significant changes in the environment to the affected parties. Therefore, an effective CSC2 system must monitor many inputs from data systems and continuously evaluate the performance of warfighting organizations against both pre-established and dynamic levels and rates. When performance falls outside established tolerance limits, an appropriate response is communicated to process owners.

It is important to emphasize that the CSC2 system is not a functional information system, e.g., a maintenance, supply, or transportation system. The CSC2 system takes parameter values from these systems but it does not create the work of transportation, e.g., transportation control numbers (TCNs), maintenance job control numbers (JCNs), or supply requisition numbers (RNs). These functional systems are used as inputs to the CSC2 system. The CSC2 system signals when the performances of these functional systems are likely to affect desired CS effects and alerts functional personnel at CS nodes to consider possible corrective actions using their functional CS systems. The CSC2 system rides above the functional systems and relates functional performance and resource levels to operational effects.

Continuously Updated Data Systems Are Needed

To increase the S&R functions of modern CSC2, measuring rates of consumption frequently will be increasingly important. The early trend recognition required for proactive support will depend on comprehending usage patterns in a timely manner. Much of the data derived from legacy systems has been shaped by "end of the month" or "end of the quarter" computations. Rates of consumption were calculated by the difference between the beginning of period levels and the end of period levels. Modern, agile warfare requires a near-real-time view of all logistics commodity and consumption data. This requires an iterative process with frequent (perhaps hourly or continuously, depending on the parameter) data updates. The traditional critical pillars of CS—fuel, munitions, food, and water—will continue to be measured, but other commodities will need to be measured and analyzed to determine how they would affect operationally relevant metrics such as deployment base initial operating capability and weapon system availability. Frequent assessment with combat-oriented analytical tools would help commanders to assess all of the potentially pacing material and support component trends. Sensing the entire support database rapidly and frequently will allow CS leadership at all levels to affect solutions to undesirable trends *before* they affect combat capability. This important feature of a robust S&R system is not found in traditional data-tracking and analysis. The CSC2 system of the future must be able to continuously monitor CS resource levels and convert that information into operational metrics; evaluate the resources needed to achieve operational goals, assess the feasibility of support options, and help to develop alternative plans; rapidly reconfigure the CS infrastructure to meet specific contingency scenario needs; employ commodity and process control metrics and process monitoring to regulate support processes; and adjust support activities during execution to optimize warfighter support.[5]

This is a large undertaking. Current and emerging information systems, which support day-to-day business processes, will likely supply the raw data needed to understand the levels and condition of materiel assets. However, in the emerging world of information systems, the "mountains of supplies" philosophy should not simply be replaced with "mountains of data" but rather with a philosophy of "the right information to the right organization at the right time." Command and control systems will need to quickly and accurately process numbers and rates of consumption into actionable correlated information packets. Using these actionable information packets, warfighters will be able to make decisions about priorities and positioning, leading to improved support architectures for varying deployed operations.

The CIRF test discussed above had several test objectives, one of which was evaluating whether the current logistics information

---

[5]   Leftwich et al. (2002).

system was adequate to support C2 decisionmaking. The test plan called for the tracking and evaluation of numerous metrics including

- customer wait time
- shop production throughput
- serviceable spare levels
- engine production flow times
- test cell pass rates
- test station status
- transportation support costs.

Metrics were assembled from within the CS disciplines of transportation, supply, and maintenance. Additionally, personnel information was monitored. One goal was to determine if current data were sufficient to cue CSC2 leadership at "trigger points" that suggest changes in structure, procedures, and manning.

At inception of the test, it was evident that no single system could report all of the required information, formatted in a way that would be easy to understand and from which adapting control decisions could be tailored. Dynamic Research Corporation (DRC), in conjunction with USAFE logistics staff, developed a single system known as the CIRF toolkit. This toolkit accumulated select data from the various stove-piped functional systems, facilitating the necessary correlation and interpretation of the vast array of data.

Although the CIRF test focused on a rather small piece of the data stream (ILM for electronic countermeasures [ECM] and LANTIRN pods, two engine types, and avionics LRUs for one MDS), it still could not correlate, analyze, and generate the essential information in a rapidly useable format. In addition to the many other valuable lessons learned in this CIRF test, the need for a layer of CSC2 analysis and presentation applications was validated.

The necessary data were located in legacy systems that had minimal interface with each other. In the absence of an interface and integration tool, data from each of these systems had to be extracted manually and collated in an ad hoc process and system. Each of the separate systems required a unique log-in procedure and separate passwords to obtain data. The requirement to adapt CSC2 data using an additional layer of application is not an indictment of the legacy systems. Each was designed to support a business process within a specific segment of the asset management chain. Most of the legacy systems effectively fulfill the role for which they were designed. However, none of them are easily adaptable to warfighter CS decisionmaking without an essential processing and accumulation effort. Significant advances in CS data systems will be required to achieve an Air Force S&RCS capability. A discussion of some of these enabling technologies is presented in Chapter Three.

Standing Combat Support Organizations

Although well-defined processes are a necessary component of the CSC2 system, standing organizations comprising trained personnel are needed to put S&RCS capabilities into action. The following section describes some of the key CS organizations identified in the CSC2 operational architecture.

Commander of the Air Force Forces Staff Forward and Rear

One key node in robust CSC2 operational architecture is the Commander of the Air Force Forces (COMAFFOR) staff, also called the Air Force Forces (AFFOR) staff. The AFFOR staff can have a component that may be deployed with the COMAFFOR. It can also have some staff who remain in the rear and serve staff functions in a reachback fashion. It will act as regional hub for monitoring, prioritizing, and allocating theater-level CS resources. It will also be responsible for mission support, base infrastructure support, and establishing movement requirements within the theater.

In general, the AFFOR Rear will be the theater integrator for commodities managed by commodity control points (CCPs). It should have complete visibility of theater resources and the authority to reconfigure them. It should receive commodity-specific information from CCPs and make integrated capability assessments (of both sortie production and facilities) and report those assessments to the A-4 who will lead the combat support element (CSE) in the Air Operations Center (AOC).[6]

Logistics Support Centers

Logistics support centers (LSCs) are key C2 nodes to the AFFOR staff. Two LSCs have been created—one to support the Combat Air Forces (CAF) and the other to support the Mobility Air Forces (MAF). These two LSCs will provide the following support functions:

- Set levels for deploying units.
- Recommend allocation of scarce spare parts based on Air Force priorities and planned requirements.
- Collect data for support assessments.
- Identify out-of-control processes for continued sustainment.
- Notify AFFOR staff of out-of-balance/control conditions that affect operational requirements.
- Request feedback and monitor/evaluate performance.
- Access options based on changing operational requirements.
- Configure spares kits.
- Identify distribution nodes both before and during deployment.

Commodity Control Points

Commodity control points will manage the supply of resources to the Major Commands (MAJCOMs), essential for the distribution of critical resources such as munitions and spares. The CCP will monitor resource inventory levels, locations, and movement information and will use these data to assess contractor and organic capabilities to meet through-put requirements. As an integrator, the CCP will bring together information from across traditional stovepipes to develop and improve feasibility and execution of plans, cost estimates, and budgets as well as to

---

[6] The distribution of A-staff functions between forward and rear COMAFFOR nodes may vary between COMAFFORs. Improved communications capability will enable increasingly more functions to be performed in the rear.

centralize buy and repair authority. It will also have the ability to allocate and reallocate cost authority during execution when priorities or conditions change. In a similar manner to the LSC, the CCPs will evaluate/ change performance when measurable thresholds fail to meet operational needs.

Supply chain managers,[7] who are key players in the CCP team, will routinely provide their information to a common electronic workspace (akin to the Air Force Portal):[8] tracking of suppliers' financial performance, forecasting demand, determining lead times and transportation and delivery routes, and developing action plans when problems arise. They will also develop contract terms and conditions for sources of supply or repair that will enable the surge actions and increased data requirements needed during wartime. They will adopt a supplier's point of view, forecasting and managing downstream problems. As with commercial firms, they will do analyses and choose suppliers based on attractiveness: What is the supplier's performance history (quality, delivery record, and price)? What is the supplier's management attitude? How well does the supplier manage technology changes? Is the supplier financially stable? The Air Force needs high-performing suppliers, and the CCP team will do rigorous evaluation and selection and then develop long-term collaborative relationships with the chosen suppliers. With guidance from Air Force headquarters, the CCP team will develop enterprise-wide strategies for those goods aligned with strategic goals and then will implement the plans and develop instruments to measure outcomes.

The LSCs will also maintain visibility of inventory levels, locations, and movement information and keep open communication with the CCPs. This information, in combination with the visibility of in-theater asset requirements, will allow the LSCs to make distribution/ redistribution decisions for spares based on Air Force operational requirements.

---

[7] The spares CCP, in addition to commodity supply chain management (SCM), will have WS-SCMs that focus on integrating information for a particular MDS.

[8] In the remainder of this monograph, we refer to this portal or system as the common electronic workspace or simply the electronic workspace

Combat Support Center

In addition to the CCPs and the AFFOR staff, a global combat support center (CSC) is another critical node. This node could be a self-contained organization with analytic capabilities or a virtual organization with analysis cells collocated with the LSCs to assess weapon system capabilities. It will act as a neutral integrator in coordination with theater A4s, LSCs, and CCPs. Moreover, this node should have responsibility for providing integrated weapon system assessments across commodities both in peacetime and in wartime. An Air Force–level cell could integrate assessments that support allocation decisions when multiple theaters are competing for the same resources and the two LSCs cannot differentiate between equal and competing priorities. The CSC could serve as the Air Force voice to the Joint Staff in any arbitration across services.

We next discuss the planning process used to assess military capabilities and the related budgeting process used to address the identified shortfalls in desired capabilities. It is important to realize that an S&RCS capability is applicable not only to the execution time frame; S&RCS also affects the components of the planning and budgeting processes associated with establishing and maintaining operating locations and those associated with supporting weapon system availability objectives.

Estimating and Budgeting for Requirements

PPBE is the current system for creating the DoD's (including all the services') contribution to the presidential budget. The system divides the budget-building process into four phases:

- planning: assesses capabilities, reviews threats, and develops guidance
- programming: translates planning guidance into achievable packages in a six-year future defense program
- budgeting: tests for feasibility of programs and creates budgets

- execution: develops performance metrics, assesses output against planned performance, and adjusts resources to achieve the desired goals.

The Program Objective Memorandum (POM) process is the critical tool of the planning phase in PPBE.[9]

The Planning Processes

There are two kinds of planning—deliberate and crisis action. Deliberate planning is an ongoing process that responds to Defense Planning Guidance (DPG) and intelligence estimates. Crisis Action Planning (CAP) parallels the deliberate processes and often borrows work that has been done to plan for conflict within a region; however, CAP is naturally more time compressed than deliberate planning. CAP must use currently available assets. Deliberate planning intends to identify asset and facility shortfalls and include them in future budgetary requirements. This section details the iterative processes that are prominent in deliberate planning and that lead to improvements in infrastructure and within CSC2 systems. It then briefly presents the CAP process, which reveals many of the same processes, but results in a beddown and support assessment. Whether deliberate or crisis action, the planning phase is the basis of all S&RCS activities. The CSC2 system of the future will measure the performance of the deployed forces against the parameters and factors that were established in the planning phase.

Deliberate Planning

During deliberate planning, Air Force planners will go through an iterative planning process similar to that portrayed in Figure 2.2. They will produce a portfolio of operational plans (potentially hundreds) with associated deployment requirements (e.g., type and number of

---

[9]   In practice, the programming and budgeting phases are combined and POM submissions are developed in conjunction with Budget Estimate Submissions (BESs), the primary tool of the budgeting phase.

aircraft, sortie rates, beddown locations). From this, AFFOR staff CS planners will produce corresponding requirements. Time-Phased Force Deployment Data (TPFDD) (what manpower and equipment, expressed as Unit Type Codes [UTCs] will be required at each base) will then be sourced and time-phased. The steps of the process are as follows:

- **Feasibility Assessment.** Feasibility will be assessed for each requirement, including manpower, equipment,[10] sustainment, and transportation, using TPFDD, visibility of AEF capabilities, beddown location, and FSL capabilities.
- **Assess Planning Options.** While planning options are being developed and updated, the CSC at the Air Staff will pass draft options on to the CCPs to get updated materiel data. The CCPs will then examine their information to determine feasibility (and resource tradeoffs if plans are not feasible) and to identify any constraints. The CSC will compile data from all CCPs to get a complete picture for each aircraft type.
- **Assess Resource Requirements.** The CSC will also analyze the effect of these resource requirements on other military requirements. Key commodities to be analyzed are spare parts, munitions, Basic Expeditionary Airfield Resources (BEAR), fuel mobility support equipment (FMSE) and fuel, and bulk commodities (food, water, and construction materials).
- **Assess Transportation Feasibility.** Global mobility is a joint issue (both in who uses it and who provides it), and the task will no doubt be accomplished by a joint organization (e.g., the U.S. Transportation Command [USTRANSCOM]), but an AFFOR Rear will estimate Air Force transportation requirements for deployment and sustainment. This whole process is iterated with modifications made to operations or CS plans, until a feasible plan is found.

---

[10] By equipment we mean non-consumables, both unit equipment and WRM, e.g., Aerospace Ground Equipment (AGE), FMSE, and vehicles.

- **Configure Infrastructure.** Comprehensive capabilities-based portfolio planning generates global requirements that will necessitate changes in the CS network to best prepare for the range of scenarios. Combat support configuration must be done at a global, strategic level to prepare the Air Force to meet future demands, including infrastructure, materiel, and personnel.
- **Analyze Beddown Possibilities.** Analysis at the Air Staff level will be done to assess global requirements for all resources, and for some, to determine how they will be postured among FSLs and FOLs.[11] The actions that follow this analysis will best prepare the Air Force for an uncertain future. Each CCP will have input into the process, but the analysis will be integrated so that resources are balanced (i.e., different resources are not postured optimally for different kinds of scenarios). For example, an output of this analysis will be how many total BEAR assets are needed and in which FSLs they should be stored.[12] This will take into account the range of scenarios, FSL and FOL maximum on Ground (MOG) and throughput constraints, travel times, and transportation limitations (e.g., ports in third world countries that will accept only high-draft seagoing vessels).
- **Purchase New Requirements.** CCPs will manage the actual purchase or repair of assets to support this global asset posturing. New contracts will be let if necessary. AFFOR staff will be the repository of data on FOL and FSL capabilities/limitations and will monitor the execution of any infrastructure additions in their AOR in support of the global posturing.
- **Develop Specific Planning Factors.** To meet each contingency plan and for steady-state requirements, planners will also establish new targets for CS MOEs. These planning factors become critical inputs to the decision support tools that provide the "look ahead" capability that enables CS to be proactive.

---

[11] This analysis should be done often enough to keep pace with changing Secretary of Defense priorities (e.g., Defense Planning Guidance) and plans, but infrequently enough to be financially feasible.

[12] Amouzegar et al. (2004).

Crisis Action Planning

Crisis action planning will essentially mirror deliberate planning, with a few exceptions. When a contingency requiring military force arises, all the strategic or long-term planning and execution activities continue in the background. Deliberate plans are made, budgets are created and executed, resources are acquired and allocated, units train, and various organizations monitor Air Force performance and capabilities.

At the outset of the crisis action planning process, as the Combatant Commander and the service components explore courses of action (COAs), AFFOR planners access the capability assessments. These assessments (e.g., beddown locations, WRM stocks, spares surge capability) form the "resource landscape" of the Air Force and inform the COA selection process. Once the Combatant Commander selects a COA, operators create an Operational Parameters Template (OPT) to jumpstart CS planning. An OPT is a single document, containing estimated operational requirements (MDS, sortie, beddown), from which CS planners will begin their CS planning. Without this single planning document, or "sheet of music," CS planners would have to make their own guesses and assumptions about operational characteristics. The CS planning process would immediately be off to an uncoordinated, haphazard start. This template is passed to AFFOR Forward and Rear nodes. AFFOR Forward planners do more situation-specific beddown planning to feed air campaign planning. Functional experts in the AFFOR Rear work from this information to create functional slices of the TPFDD. After the pieces are assembled, AFFOR Rear planners source the forces.

The Programming and Budgeting Processes

The MAJCOMs submit programs in the form of a POM to a body on the Air Staff called the Air Force Corporate Structure. The resources covered in the POM refer mainly to manpower, facilities, weapon systems, and operating funds. Although it is advertised as a biennial process (with an update of the budget only in the second year), in practice, the dynamics of DoD force a compilation every year. This means that in any one year, the process has four overlapping budget positions in various stages of development. The PPBE transforms military plans into programs to carry out the plans, creating the Future Years Defense Program (FYDP) for two budget years and five out-years and then providing the cost of those programs to Congress for approval and funding. The FYDP is a database tool that keeps DoD management informed of what has been accomplished in the recent past and what is slated for funding and accomplishment in the short to medium term. The FYDP represents how DoD money will be obligated in future years based on plans and obligations approved by the Office of the Secretary of Defense (OSD) during previous PPBE cycles.[13]

The Role of Commodity Control Points in Budgeting

The CCPs are key resource management nodes that should play a major role in Air Force cost estimation. The deliberate planning described above will establish requirements for many commodities directly, and each CCP will perform cost estimates of global requirements for its commodity to feed the Air Force POM process.

When it comes to day-to-day budget execution, the CCP is the focal point, supporting units and maintaining a healthy supply chain. The CCP will direct the flow of information, products, services, and financial management for its commodity. It will track the constraints in capacity, expertise, funding, and human resources, routinely providing data and analysis to the common electronic workspace. Currently, CCPs use EXPRESS (Execution and Prioritization of Repair Support System) to make depot repair decisions based on current Air Force needs. Another approach, called Advanced Planning and Scheduling (APS) (see Chapter Four for more information), is currently being tested at the Oklahoma City Air Logistics Center (ALC) and provides a more integrated, responsive, and near-real-time approach to the planning and assessment of repair decisions based on operational plans. Additionally, the CCP will operate within a network of collaborative relationships. For spares, for instance, sister organizations at the Air

---

[13] For detailed information on PPBE process, see Snyder et al. (2006); and Camm and Lewis (2003).

Force Materiel Command (AFMC) such as the Warfighter Sustainment Division will provide resident maintenance, supply, munitions, transportation, and logistics plans expertise when needed. The CSC at the Air Staff will provide liaison to the joint community and will be the conduit for Air Force plans, policies, and priorities. The logistics support communities at the MAJCOMs will serve as the CCPs' direct link to the warfighters.

The CCP will also manage the allocation of cost authority across weapon systems to the Supply Chain Manager for both procurement and maintenance. The basis of the weapon system buy lists and repair actions will initially be the full requirement, but when cost authority is released and turns out to be less than budgeted, the CCP will reallocate according to MAJCOM/Air Force headquarters priorities. Revised buy lists and repair actions will then be generated and executed. Whether or not full cost authority is received, closed-loop feedback mechanisms will be developed to track the execution of the cost authority to determine if operational goals are being met. If the feedback results show that execution is not working well and analysis determines that another allocation could better support availability goals, the CCP will have the ability to reallocate cost authority.

The Execution Processes

The CSC2 system also plays a key role in the execution stage, across deployment, employment, and sustainment to redeployment and reconstitution.

Deployment
The AFFOR staff is a major focal point of information flow and decisionmaking for the deployment process. The AFFOR Forward, with specific knowledge of its area of responsibility (AOR), performs beddown planning. The AFFOR Rear handles TPFDD development, and the Forward element then monitors force reception. Deploying units have visibility of the TPFDD and when and what they must deploy. Although USTRANSCOM plans the lift, the AFFOR Rear manages

the connection between USTRANSCOM and deploying units, ensuring communication and solving problems when they arise (e.g., if the unit is unable to deploy). The AFFOR Forward communicates initial force reception information on each FOL to the AOC. As deployment continues, even after the start of operations, the AFFOR Forward continues to monitor and report force reception information to the AOC/ CSE. The AFFOR Forward would liaison with the AFFOR Rear to help solve beddown problems as they occur.

Employment/Sustainment

The major CS activity during employment and sustainment is monitoring performance. Low-level metrics are monitored and fed into the CSC2 system, allowing for the computation of high-level metrics that are monitored to drive allocation and planning decisions. FOLs monitor metrics such as spares levels, repair times, munitions levels, and infrastructure condition and capabilities. The AFFOR staff monitors and integrates these metrics and plans get-well actions when actual performance violates tolerance limits. The AFFOR Rear monitors the Theater Distribution System (TDS) and plans adjustments as necessary.

The CSC monitors force-level metrics and arbitrates when resource decisions cannot be decided within a theater. CCPs supply commodity resources, monitor processes, and report performance. Consider munitions as an example. The FOLs monitor stocks and report their status. The AFFOR staff observes FOL and WRM stock levels and CCP information and reports status and problems to the AOC for planning. Similar integration is done for spares. FOLs and CIRFs monitor stock levels and repair times. The AFFOR staff integrates these with delivery times and works with the LSCs and CCPs to ensure adequate spares support.

Capability Assessment and Reporting

A major feature of a robust CSC2 architecture is a comprehensive capability assessment and reporting system. Planning for contingencies and configuring the CS infrastructure and resources are tasks that need to be done, but to complete the feedback loop, CS capabilities must be measured and compared to planned levels. Without accurate knowledge of its resource capabilities, the Air Force will be unable to mitigate shortfalls and may be caught unawares when a contingency arises.

Assessing Performance Shortfalls

Periodically,[14] organizational nodes will assess their performance in supporting operations and project their ability to meet DoD requirements. These projections include bottlenecks in achieving goals, time to correct deficiencies, and new or reallocated funding that could alleviate the problems. The CSC receives all CCP assessments and projections and presents periodic updates to the Air Staff, along with problems and proposed get-well plans. For instance, the personnel CCP will report on the readiness levels of its UTCs. If some UTCs required for contingency operations are not mission-capable,[15] or fully deployable, the CCP (working with the MAJCOMs) will propose get-well actions such as alternative UTCs or units or training that would bring the UTC to full capability in an adequate time frame. The spares CCP will periodically determine when projected operational performance deviates from plans, determine the causes of the deviation, and test alternative get-well approaches, including reallocating funds. The munitions CCP will check the levels of its munitions (this is especially important if current contingency operations are depleting stores of critical munitions) and their capabilities and the throughput of its ammo dumps, especially if any infrastructure changes have been made since the plans were formed. CCPs will centrally manage other WRM (e.g., BEAR, vehicles) and will provide global visibility over each resource. These capabilities will be widely available to Air Force leaders. CCP cells will

---

[14] Capability assessment cycles should be created and tailored for each capability—and should occur often enough to keep up with the pace of changes but not so frequently that they become time- or cost-prohibitive.

[15] ART (AEF UTC reporting tool), the Air Force's tool for reporting and monitoring AEF UTC readiness, uses a stoplight scheme to rate the readiness of UTCs. Green means fully mission-capable (according to UTC mission-capable statement), yellow means partially mission-capable but still able to meet the mission capability requirement. Red means not mission-capable and unable to meet specified requirements.

enter detailed information into a common electronic workspace, and much of the aggregation, capability assessment, and reporting will be done by automated programs.

Information Security and the Access to Information

Such an increasingly precise capability assessment and reporting system presents new security risks. Once the Air Force analyzes and expresses its capabilities with this level of fidelity (e.g., quantifying how many sorties will be lost at FOLs if a backlog occurs at a particular transportation hub), it then possesses information valuable to its own planners as well as to its enemies. A system for capabilities analysis and reporting must have security adequate to protect this information. This subject will be discussed in more detail in Chapter Three.

CHAPTER THREE

Tools and Technology Requirements for Sense and Respond Combat Support

Previous chapters presented the argument that a CSC2 system combined with certain information technologies is the way to achieve an S&RCS capability for the Air Force. We believe that in the near term, Air Force S&RCS can be more effectively achieved by focusing on the implementation of these technologies into the CSC2 architecture. Both the recent overall DoD transformation effort and the Force-Centric Logistics Enterprise (FLE)[1] literature have recognized the concept of S&RL as a key building block of ACS. Current technology has enabled a limited set of the sense and respond capabilities posited in concept and architectural documents; however, their full implementation remains dependent on substantial future technological development, as well as other conceptual transformation discussed above. In this chapter, we present a brief review of the current state of S&RL-related technology and concepts in the DoD (including DoD Office of Force Transformation initiatives, the Defense Advanced Research Projects Agency [DARPA], the Air Force Research Laboratories

---

[1] The Force-Centric Logistics Enterprise comprehends that logistics is not an "end"; rather, logistics needs to be continuously tied to operational outcomes. Assessments of logistics performance need to be likewise tied, not to internal management measures of merit alone but primarily to operational goals that were developed in the planning stages and are continuously changing with battlefield conditions. FLE shifts the focus and emphasis of logistics data analysis from an internal orientation to an external (operational) one. For more information, see *Logistics and Materiel Quarterly Newsletter* (2003).

[AFRL] study, the private sector, and research institutions). We conclude with a discussion of the road ahead for S&RL technological development. The goal of this chapter is to survey some of the necessary S&RL technologies and ascertain their current maturity, with particular regard to Air Force S&RCS requirements.

The Office of Force Transformation Program

The DoD OFT has attempted to develop a unified concept for military S&RL. It is useful to review that statement here:

> Sense and Respond Logistics is a system interwoven with network-centric operations and based upon highly adaptive, self-synchronizing, dynamically reconfigurable demand and support networks that anticipate and stimulate actions to enhance capability or mitigate support shortfalls.[2]

OFT addresses S&RL from a DoD-wide perspective, i.e., a joint force perspective, and as an important component of DoD's focused logistics strategy. As stated in the S&RL concept document, OFT only promotes and facilitates "the continuous development and refinement of concepts, processes, technologies, and organizations in order to start influencing change immediately."[3] OFT considered architectural development planning that includes technology views as well as the development of an information technology (IT) S&RL prototype.

One of these architectural concepts is the Integrated Enterprise Domain Architecture (IEDA), which has the objectives of integrating, accommodating, and employing concepts and components of logistics, operations, and intelligence architectures and of their command, control, communications, computers, intelligence, surveillance, and reconnaissance (C4ISR) concepts.[4] Presently, IEDA is in a pre-

---

[2] U.S. Department of Defense (2004a).

[3] U.S. Department of Defense (2004a).

[4] U.S. Department of Defense (2004b).

development stage, but plans are to eventually link it to other architectures or programs, including Joint Staff J-4, Joint Forces Command (JFCOM), U.S. Marine Corps (USMC), USTRANSCOM, and possibly certain organizations in the Navy and the Army. Among the in-work project linkages is the RAND–Air Force CSC2 operational architecture (OA) as the Air Force vehicle for coordinating with concepts in S&RL. Overall, the OFT program for S&RL is in a very early stage, but it has the potential to influence and effect near- to midterm changes in some current programs using today's S&RL technologies, and tomorrow's, as they become available. OFT suggests that elements of the concept can be employed in an evolutionary development in the very near term and could result in immediate operational gains.[5]

OFT has also examined some of the nontechnical issues that require maturation concurrent with tool development. These include policy issues, acquisition strategies, the need for human factor studies to determine the effects of using technology to reduce the human cognitive burden, how to bring convergence among all efforts, and how to influence leaders to accept changes to make co-evolution and integration possible, to name a few.[6] A recent DoD-sponsored forum[7] examined the special issues inherent in such lateral redistribution of materiel and identified several complicating factors that will need to be addressed once the technical barriers to S&RL are removed. Some of these issues will require policy changes to areas such as payment and reconciliation; others addressed difficulties in the joint C2 environment. One of the group's key conclusions was that unless significant improvements are made to "last-mile" transportation in-theater, S&RL will have a limited effect on operations.

---

[5] U.S. Department of Defense (2004b). In conversations with OFT staff, the time frame for identifying and developing specific technologies for full implementation of all elements of operational S&RL is 2010 to 2015.

[6] Private communication with OFT principal staff.

[7] Joint Logistics Transformation Forum (2005).

Sense and Respond Technical Requirements

Numerous initiatives and programs are under way to develop the technology necessary to implement the S&RL concepts. Although there is a great diversity among proposed approaches to S&RL implementation and its applications, a general theme is best stated by the IBM Sense and Respond Enterprise Team.[8] This group believes that technologies and innovation to support S&R must have[9]

- the ability to detect, organize, and analyze pertinent information and sense critical business (force) conditions
- the filters for enterprise data to enable stable responses to disturbances in the business (military) environment
- the intelligent response agents that analyze global value chain relationships and information and derive the optimal strategy for the best supply chain performance
- predictive modeling at multiple levels: strategic, tactical, and operational
- agent coordination mechanisms at multiple levels: strategic, tactical, and operational
- the ability to learn by comparing previously predicted trends with recorded data and information to improve future responses
- a software infrastructure to integrate heterogeneous and collaborative agents implementing critical business policies and making operational decisions.

The IBM concept of S&RL can be contrasted with the OFT perspective. OFT, within its All Views Architecture, lists specific systems architecture components for S&RL, including the following capabilities:[10]

---

[8]   Lin et al. (2002).

[9]   It is interesting to note that these requirements are in line with RAND's CSC2 concepts, which the Air Force is implementing.

[10]   U.S. Department of Defense (2004b).

- **passive and active tagging, instruments, and sensors** that provide location status, diagnoses, prognoses, and other information relative to operations space entities, especially for conditions and behavior that affect force capabilities management, logistics, and sustainment.
- **intelligent software agents** that represent operations space entities, conditions, and behaviors, provide a focus for control of action or behavior, or act as monitors.
- **S&RL knowledge bases** oriented toward force capabilities management, logistics, and sustainment.
- **S&RL reference data,** again focused on force capabilities, assets, and resources related to force capabilities management, logistics, and sustainment.
- **S&RL rule sets,** which govern the operations and organization of S&RL functions, activities, and transactions.
- **S&RL cognitive decision support tools** uniquely supporting force capabilities management, logistics, and sustainment.
- **unique S&RL processes, applications, portals, and interfaces** not provided by either Distributed Adaptive Operations Command and Control (DAO C2) or the Network-Centric Operations and Warfare (NCOW) infrastructure.

These are representative of the technologies and innovations that have been identified with military and commercial S&RL initiatives. In the next section, we discuss two important technologies needed to enable an ultimate S&RCS capability: radio frequency identification (RFID) and intelligent (adaptive) software agents.[11]

Radio Frequency Identification

Radio frequency identification is both a military and a commercial technology program. As a DoD program, it encompasses a family of automatic identification technology (AIT) capabilities that sup-

---

[11] This certainly is not an inclusive list because this is an active research area with numerous initiatives across the globe. Although we will examine a few of these in some detail, projecting the availability of these technologies is beyond the scope of our research.

port hands-off processing of materiel transactions. DoD RFID policy, issued in October 2003, requires use of active RFID tags on aerial pallets and containers immediately, and use of passive RFID tags on warehouse pallets and cartons by January 2005.[12] Technically, RFID offers a way to identify unique items using radio waves. Typically, a reader communicates with a tag, which holds digital information in a microchip. However, some chipless forms of RFID tags use material to reflect back a portion of the radio waves beamed at them. This technology is of equal interest to military and commercial enterprises.

In the future, RFID or its next-generation technology may be ubiquitous in the supply chain. This and other similar technology, along with process and procedural improvements, will allow commercial enterprise retailers to know the location of replenishments in real time, helping them respond to potential out-of-stocks before they occur. Manufacturers would know the demand for their products in real time, enabling them to react to changes immediately and achieve efficiencies never before possible. Manufacturers would also be able to do mass customization, because software could automatically monitor the location and flow of the hundreds of different parts and materials that go into their products—something very difficult to do when the bar codes on all components have to be scanned manually. These RFID-enabled capabilities are equally important to military enterprises.

Experience from recent conflicts is replete with incidences of large stocks en route to the theater becoming unidentifiable and their disposition delayed until they were physically inspected and combat units began to identify critical shortages, often affecting warfighting capability. There are also several examples of real-time information-gathering and distribution. For example, in Iraq, some Marine units had active tags not just on pallets but also on vehicles. RFID readers were set up at a distribution center in Kuwait, at the Iraq-Kuwait border, and at checkpoints along the main arteries in Iraq. When trucks passed the readers, the location of the goods they were carrying was updated in the DoD's In-Transit Visibility (ITV) network database. This enabled

---

[12] Joint Chiefs of Staff (2004), p. 75.

commanders on the ground to see the precise location of the replenishments needed to sustain operations.[13] RFID implementation is limited, but the DoD goal is to minimize human involvement when collecting data on shipments and their movements. Scanning RFID tags allows the automatic acquisition of identification and location data for shipments, leading to increased data accuracy and more rapid movement of goods. Eventually, RFID information will be integrated with enterprise and supply chain systems so that information can be available where needed. Some experts see RFID, along with other real-time technologies such as sensory networks and global positioning system (GPS), as bringing changes that will be every bit as profound as those produced by the Internet. The pervasive use of RFID technology does not depend on the S&RL concept retaining a place of importance in OFT planning. The attainment of S&RL concepts, however, may be difficult or nearly impossible without RFID technology.

Software Agents and Agent-Based Modeling

The application of "agent technology" in S&RL research has become pervasive both in military and nonmilitary programs. In this section, we briefly describe agent-based modeling, applications of agents and agent-based modeling, and the use of agents in S&RL.[14]

What Is an Agent?

Decades ago, the fundamental unit of software was a complete program. Code and data occupied the same logical and physical space, and the code did not have logical divisions (i.e., everything was connected, possibly even by arbitrary go-to statements), so programmers effectively determined the behavior of the entire program before it began execution. This "monolithic" software evolved to more modular structured code, wherein each subroutine (or "function") was

---

[13] Roberti (2005).

[14] For a more detailed discussion of agent based modeling see Epstein (1999); and Illachinski (2004).

encapsulated, its state supplied externally through global parameters passed to the function, and its control invoked externally by a function call.[15]

Object-oriented programming further localized code to include within an object both its functions and the variables it manipulated, formalizing the protocol for persistent storage of data within a function. Software agents take the next step, localizing not only functionality and data but also control. Entities known as agents, controlled by decisionmaking algorithms, can execute many local interactions resulting in the emergence of global behaviors. That is, agents are not under the control of the program—they do not follow orders, but rather have strong autonomous characteristics that distinguish them from other software paradigms. Each agent retains its own functions and methods, so that other software entities cannot freely cause those functions to be executed. As a result of this autonomy, agents exhibit complex social behavior, whereby one agent may attempt to "persuade" another agent to execute a particular function. The agents interacting in the system can be designed to receive feedback and adapt accordingly, so one agent in pursuit of its own goal could attempt to cause a positive reaction by another agent.[16] Agents typically are proactive (goal-directed and thus intentional) or reactive, have abilities to communicate or negotiate with each other, learn from experience, adapt to changes in their environments, make plans, and reason (e.g., via logic or game theory).[17] The agents often interact in a self-adaptive, nonlinear manner with each time step. This self-adaptive behavior creates a vast number of variables and facilitates research into emergent behaviors. The aggregate effects of the myriad of individual decisions can be studied, for a given scenario, to assess the effects on the whole system.[18]

---

[15] Parunak (1999).

[16] Perugini et al. (2002).

[17] Davidsson et al. (2004).

[18] Wolf (2003a).

Agent-Based Modeling

Although individual automated software agents are already employed commercially for particular tasks, intelligent multiagent systems are still in early development.[19] Consequently, agent-based models (ABMs) have historically had only a limited effect on practical decisionmaking and only in recent years have academic researchers explored the use of intelligent agents for supply chain management.[20]

Although ABMs are properly understood as multiagent systems, not all agents or multiagent systems are employed for modeling and simulation purposes. Several researchers, including some under DoD contracts, have developed applications of ABMs for SCM.[21]

Applications of Agents and Agent-Based Modeling

Agents have been used in telecommunications, e-commerce, transportation, electric power networks, and manufacturing processes. Within telecommunications, software agents bear the responsibility for error-checking (e.g., dropped packets), routing and retransmission, and load-balancing over the network. Web search robots are agents that traverse Web sites collecting information and cataloging their results. When a customer searches for an item on a merchant's Web site, at the bottom of the page there may be a list of similar products that other customers interested in the item also viewed. Similar agents assemble customized news reports and filter spam from email. Data-mining agents seek trends and patterns in an abundance of information from varying sources and are of particular interest for all-source intelligence analysis.[22]

Agents have also been used for scheduling in manufacturing and to generate, evaluate, and modify candidate solutions for off-line optimization procedures.

---

[19] A multiagent system is a collection of agents cooperating or competing with each other to fulfill common and individual goals (see Davidsson et al., 2004).

[20] Lempert (2002).

[21] See for example, Parunak (1999).

[22] Hollywood et al. (2004).

Ideal applications of agent technology exhibit the following characteristics:[23]

- **Modularity.** Agents are best suited to applications that fall into natural modules. An agent has its own set of state variables, distinct from those of the environment, but its input and output mechanisms couple its state variables to some subset of the environment's state variables.
- **Decentralization.** The decentralized nature of agents makes them well suited to applications that can be decomposed into stand-alone processes, each capable of doing useful things without continuous direction by a central authority. Decentralization minimizes the effect of errors or changes in one module to other modules in the system.
- **Ill-defined structure.** When the structure of the system is underspecified or subject to change, agent technology permits reconfiguration without starting "from scratch."
- **Complexity.** Colloquially, the whole is more than the sum of its component parts. Complex systems frequently exhibit feedback interactions or other nonlinear behavior, path-dependence, and nested structure.

A computer's operating system (OS) is an example of a multiagent system. The OS controls resources and manages competing demands through a system of agents that monitor and assign resources. Although the OS gives control of certain resources to a program (and thus does not control those resources while they are in use), it can terminate a program for violating resource rules (i.e., a segmentation fault). The OS thus might serve as an analog for military logistics management.

ABMs are ideally used to model interactions between the heterogeneous behaviors of individual (autonomous) decisionmaking entities.[24] These actors may be characterized by their unique situations

---

[23] Parunak (1999).

[24] Bonabeau (2002).

within the system being modeled, their differing information about themselves or the state of the system, and their differing decision rules or strategies. ABMs can readily be applied to system dynamics problems in business and organization processes. ABMs bring the "naturalness" advantage (which allows more natural application of adaptive techniques to control the system), but in many regimes physics-based models would be sufficient and would consume less time and computational resources. For large numbers of actors that are heterogeneous in their position (information set) and decision rules, the aggregation and formal assumptions required for a comprehensible set of partial differential equations can yield less realistic results than can be achieved via agent-based modeling.[25]

Exploring Sensitivity to Assumptions and Random Variations in Behavior

By incorporating these individual differences (micromotives) into an interacting system of agents, one might observe surprising system-level outcomes (macrobehaviors).[26] By definition, emergent system-level behavior cannot be reduced to (or deduced from) the sum of the individual behaviors. The difference occurs in the interactions between the individuals. For example, one might observe that many scenarios (e.g., changing the information and decision rules of the actors) lead to similar outcomes or that similar scenarios lead to very different outcomes. Thus, ABMs allow the modeler to explore the sensitivity of the model's outcomes to assumptions made about the individual actors and their behaviors. ABMs can also be used to predict a range of possible outcomes that might be generated when the behavior of individual actors is inherently unpredictable (e.g., when each actor's decision rule must be drawn from a distribution) or is affected by learning and adaptation.

Exploring Cooperation and Competition in Organizations

Game theory demonstrates that rational actors who base their behavior on the behavior of others can generate suboptimal, noncoopera-

---

[25] Hengartner and Blume-Kohout (2006).

[26] Schelling (1978).

tive outcomes. ABMs permit the exploration of incentives to promote cooperation among actors with varying information and motivations, under competitive pressures. ABMs are natural formal representations for human social systems.

Within computational organization science, agents (human and artificial) are both consumers and producers of knowledge. Humans and the socio-technical systems in which they function are not fundamentally rational (in the economic sense of the term) but instead are limited in their abilities to manage and process information, and satisfy or approximate the best solutions.[27] The information available to an individual agent is a function of its position within a network.

Agent-Based Modeling for Sense and Respond Logistics

ABMs are already in wide use within the DoD for force-on-force simulations but have only recently been adapted for military logistics use. The logistics domain is distributed and involves decentralized (autonomous) organizations. These organizations are also

- intentional entities, with goals (functions and roles) and beliefs, using processes and expertise to achieve their goals
- reactive, and thus responsive to changes that occur in their environment
- social, so they interact with other organizations to achieve their goals, where the social interaction is typically complex, such as negotiation, rather than just action requests.

The similarity in characteristics between agents and organizations makes agents an appropriate choice for modeling organizations. This also explains agent functionality in carrying out organizational or human processes in S&RL applications. Moreover, robust distributed C2 strategies can also be tested using ABMs.[28] Although some simple supply chain simulations have been done for logistics,

---

[27] Carley (2002).

[28] Bonabeau, Hunt, and Gaudiano (2003).

almost none have modeled actual organizations with the requisite detail and calibration necessary to compare alternative policies and gain insight.

In summary, one may want to use ABMs when[29]

- **Individual behavior is nonlinear and can be characterized by discrete decisions, thresholds, if-then rules, or nonlinear coupling.** Describing discontinuity in individual behavior is difficult with differential equations. For example, if a logistics officer orders parts in batches, he may have a threshold for making parts requests (rather than continuously demanding replacements for parts used).
- **History matters.** Path-dependence, lagging responses, non-Markovian behavior, or temporal correlations including learning and adaptation are applicable to the system.
- **Averages are not good enough.** Under certain conditions, small fluctuations in a complex system can be amplified, so that the system is stable for incremental changes but unstable to large perturbations.

It should be noted, however, that agent-based modeling is subject to many limitations and weaknesses, such as the difficulty in ascertaining a complete picture of an agent's behavior given the complexity of the system. More important is the external or operational validity of the model—can it accurately and adequately match the real world that it is trying to simulate?

DoD S&RL Initiatives

We next present several recent and current DoD initiatives to develop S&RL capabilities.

---

[29] Bonabeau (2002).

DARPA Research and Development

DARPA has been working on an end-to-end logistics system under the Advanced Logistics Project (ALP).[30] Under this project, DARPA developed an advanced agent architecture with applications to logistics. As follow-on to ALP, DARPA initiated a program called Ultra-Log that attempted to introduce robust, secure, and scalable logistics agents into the architecture. Ultra-Log is an information technology suite with the following characteristics:[31]

- It includes a survivable logistics information system that maintains continuity of operations while under extreme stress.
- It offers a strategy for technical success that treats survivability as an emergent property. It should develop a distributed agent-based interoperable system of systems that provides security, robustness, and scalability.
- It works under the assumption that the best practices of operating systems and network security frequently fail. It offers a balance tradeoff between security, scalability, and robustness.

Ultra-Log ultimately is seeking valid applications to DoD problems (e.g., Defense Logistics Institute applications) while adopting commercial open-source models. Consequently, DARPA considered an open-source technology offered under a cognitive agent architecture (Cougaar) platform. Cougaar is a Java-based architecture for the construction of large-scale distributed agent-based applications.[32] DARPA used Cougaar to assess the feasibility of using advanced agent-based technology to conduct rapid, large-scale, distributed logistics planning, as well as for testing the survivability of such distributed agent-based systems operating in extremely chaotic environments. Through DARPA's initiative, Cougaar's architecture and agents were adopted

---

[30] Information on DARPA's research is based on personal communications with Dr. Mark Greaves, the current Ultra-Log program manager; see also DARPA's Web site, www.darpa.gov.

[31] Defense Advanced Projects Agency (n.d.).

[32] For more information on Cougaar, see www.cougaar.org.

by defense contractors for use in both production and development programs.

S&RL Demonstration—U.S. Army

DARPA and the U.S. Army Logistics Transformation Agency (LTA), the Army's lead for S&RL, provided an example demonstrating how far DARPA agent technology transfer takes a potential user toward implementing an S&RL capability.[33] This demonstration of S&RL was designed to illustrate the "state-of-the-possible" using Cougaar-based technology in an actual setting with a limited unit, weapon system thread, and actual data and information. This demonstration, not unlike other prototype systems, covered a spectrum of capabilities (although greatly restricted in scope) using agents, sensors, communications, and other essential S&R enablers in a very limited scenario.

The Army LTA managers' intent was for this to lead to the development of an adaptive logistics C2 capability, which, as stressed throughout this monograph, is the proper focus for S&RCS efforts.

Coalition Agent eXperiment

Coalition Agent eXperiment (CoAX), another DARPA project, is an example of the utility of agent technology for military logistics planning. A Multi-Agent Logistics Tool (MALT), implemented within CoAX, was developed using agent technology to have agents represent organizations within the logistics domain and model their logistics functions, processes, expertise, and interactions with other organizations.[34] Agents in MALT cooperate with each other to form a distributed logistics plan (with services from various organizations) to meet their logistics goals. Because this was a coalition program, it involved more than one organization, and one main finding was that a centralized agent planning approach might not be appropriate when different organizations with conflicting self-interests are involved. In a decentralized system, conflict resolution would be embedded within the

---

[33] USA Log Transformation Agency (2005).

[34] CoAX attracted over 20 organizations from the United States, United Kingdom, and Australia (see Perugini et al., 2002).

negotiation processes. One technical limitation of centralization had to do with coalition agents having to communicate a large quantity of information to the central agent for processing, whereas in a decentralized approach, agents could process the information themselves and send only the results of their analysis.

The project generated important lessons for S&RL. The authors emphasized two types of issues that need to be overcome for agents to be effectively used for military logistics planning—technological and social (human acceptability). We believe that the issues are the same for use in executing logistics functions. Under technology, the identified issues include logistics business process modeling, protocols, ontologies, automated information-gathering, and security. We found some of these being addressed in DARPA's work. Under social acceptability, the following were important: trusting agents to do business for you, accountability and the law, humans and agents working together, efficiency metrics, ease of use, adjustable autonomy, adjustable visibility, and social acceptability versus optimality.

Map Aware Non-Uniform Automata

The Map Aware Non-Uniform Automata (MANA) program is an example of the use of an agent-based model to simulate logistics issues in a humanitarian assistance/disaster relief operation.[35] This experiment included relevant CS parameters to the HA/DR model such as response lag and mobility. Although this experience highlighted the limitations of existing ABMs for applications in CS, it showed new avenues for the military use of a system-level model that integrates reachback to CONUS with the competing demands of agents.

S&RL Information Technology Prototype

The S&RL information technology prototype was originally developed by OFT to advance understanding of the S&RL model throughout the DoD. Building the IT prototype provided developers with an opportunity to integrate new and legacy decision support tools, map-based visualization techniques, Web portals, and an Enterprise Application

---

[35] Wolf (2003b).

Integration (EAI) framework, all riding on top of a real-time information bus architecture. DARPA suggested the use of intelligent agents to help manage the complexity of the many nodes that simultaneously consume and provide resources throughout the network. A business rule engine was integrated with the combined Predictive Support Awareness (PSA) hybrid capabilities and intelligent agents.[36] The prototype was first used by the Air Force Materiel Command's PSA program, which was identified as having many of the technical elements of the IT prototype. PSA sought to optimize the Air Force supply chain with one end anchored to AFMC and the other directly to the warfighters in the field, in an attempt to improve both the prediction of logistics needs and problems as well as the resolution of problems in advance of their identification by end users.

The updated prototype caught the interest of U.S. Marine Corps proponents who wanted to construct a demonstration similar to the Army's, using the IT prototype. The value of the prototype for this investigation was to see another state-of-the-possible demonstration of core IT technologies within a hybrid S&RL system, tested in a more realistic (but still very limited) USMC scenario. The IT prototype included a net-centric view, used intelligent agents as proxies and facilitators for people to help manage automated logistics processes where appropriate, and contained a business rule engine to facilitate end-user creation, modification, and management of applicable business rules. An important feature of this prototype was that its core technologies (including portals, graphic user interfaces, and agents) were all commercial off-the-shelf (COTS) technologies.

Some of the prototype's features that were highlighted during the USMC scenario demonstration enabled a better understanding of S&RL components and their activities. Example features included network-viewable components (portal, map interface, digital dashboard stoplight tools) for network and agent behavior monitoring, and decision support aids and metrics analysis/monitoring to facilitate trend and performance analysis. This demonstration presented intelligent agent activity and interaction, with both other agents and humans,

---

[36] This proposed program effort was briefed to AFMC/CV and was well received.

when help was needed (or desired) to manage nonautonomous issues or to resolve conflicts. Finally, the demonstration showed how Cougaar/Ultra-Log–based plug-ins and their associated business rules defined each agent's "personality." Given its origin and subsequent uses, the IT prototype appears to be consistent with the goal of the co-evolutionary experimentation thread expressed in the OFT concept document. The OFT, AFMC, and Marine Corps investments described here could be leveraged to further develop S&RL capabilities to facilitate understanding, acceptance, and early implementation of S&RCS.

Human Factor Aspects of S&RL

The Air Force Research Laboratory, Logistics Readiness Branch (AFRL/HEAL) has focused its attention on human factor issues in S&RL, with a concentration on cognitive decision support.[37] Because of the growing interest in leveraging collaboration technologies to support distributed operations in initiatives such as S&RL and NCW, DoD is giving considerable attention to the testing of collaboration technologies through programs such as the Defense Collaboration Tool Suite (DCTS). However, the emphasis of the testing associated with these technologies or applications is primarily from an IT perspective against well-defined requirements or standards. A full consideration of the human aspects of such systems is lacking; there has been insufficient study of how collaborative technologies or Computer Supported and Cooperative Work (CSCW) applications improve or impede human performance in distributed environments involving collaboration between warfighters.[38] AFRL proposes to address this gap by researching and developing enhanced or novel methodologies and measures to evaluate the effect of collaboration technologies on human performance from an individual, team, and organizational perspective. This group suggests that human performance metrics should be created along with other performance metrics for S&RL functions and

---

[37] Personal communication with Mr. Edward Boyle, Chief, AFRL/HEAL.

[38] Team-Based Assessment of Socio-Technical Logistics (TASL) point paper, AFRL/HEAL.

activities in the military enterprise, although such considerations are currently not being called for in the requirements.

Autonomic Logistics

Autonomic logistics (AL) has been described as "a broad term used to describe technologies that predict failure in operating systems, monitor stockage levels in consumables, automatically report impending failures and order replacements without human intervention."[39]

The military origin of the AL concept stems from early Joint Strike Fighter (JSF) F-35 procurement, complementing AFRL's work in the 1990s on integrating and automating maintenance data collection with maintenance operations. As originally conceived, AL replicated the human body's autonomic nervous system, which monitors, controls, and adjusts one's autonomic response to external stimuli.

According to the JSF program, AL is required to be a seamless, embedded solution that integrates current performance, operational parameters, current configuration, scheduled upgrades and maintenance, component history, predictive diagnostics (prognostics) and health management, and service support into a system that includes mission planning and an integrated product data management system.[40] In a simulated setting, it was demonstrated how a network of computers and aircraft sensors on board an F-35 would trigger an autonomic response to a pending maintenance action. If a failure occurs or is predicted to occur, the Joint Distributed Information System would facilitate a series of actions to provide the appropriate repair information and replacement parts to the right maintainer. Human interaction is thus minimized as data flow from the air vehicle through the maintenance infrastructure and ultimately to the Boeing F-35 supplier community.[41]

The AL concept, with its combination of current technologies for real-time monitoring of systems in the field (such as RFID) and advanced prediction tools to forecast future needs, aims to take

---

[39] Menotti (2004).

[40] See the Joint Strike Fighter Program Web site, www.jsf.mil.

[41] Boeing (2000).

required actions in advance of crises. Long-term predictions are still required for strategic planning purposes, as well as for processes with long lead times. However, as more real-time information becomes available, the status of every part at every location can be monitored. This allows other prediction capabilities to focus on near-term requirements, reducing uncertainty and allowing improved decisionmaking and prognostic-based intervention.

AL aspects such as a prognostic and health management (PHM) system have been used on Army and Navy helicopters. However, an AL capability is applicable not only to new weapon systems. The implementation of a robust S&RCS capability will require AL applications on some judiciously chosen existing weapon system platforms, necessitating extensive and costly retrofitting. The benefits accrued through the AL concept must be closely weighed against these retrofit costs on both a system-by-system and a total capability basis.

Commercial and University Initiatives

The following section discusses some commercial and university initiatives that have developed some of the technologies needed to enable an S&RCS capability and presents a number of industrial applications of fielded S&R systems.

IBM Sense and Respond Programs and Technology

The IBM Sense and Respond (SAR) Blue program was a major influence on the military OFT enterprise definition. The primary tenet of the IBM approach is that a successful S&R system has to employ careful planning as well as intelligence, flexibility, and responsiveness in execution. Additional analytical capabilities are needed to enhance a pure S&R model that may fall into chaotic situations and not achieve high levels of distributed efficiency. IBM's system was designed to address this need. It is a hybrid of the S&R and the make-and-sell models, combining analytical data-mining, planning, and optimization technologies. The IBM SAR system implements an adaptive S&R philosophy and can detect and use the most appropriate management policies in a given business context. This hybrid and adaptive model enables the enterprise to use the best model for efficiency and responsiveness under different situations and achieve a balanced business performance.[42] The technologies and key innovations that support this enterprise are listed above, and are similar to those identified by the OFT enterprise.

IBM has invested $250 million in the development of a standards-based infrastructure to support an S&R environment, committing nearly 1,000 consultants and developers to focus on the rollout of industry-specific solutions for its customers.[43] Perhaps most relevant to any military application of S&RL is IBM's Agent Building and Learning Environment (ABLE), a Java-based framework, component library, and productivity toolkit for building COTS intelligent agents using machine-learning and reasoning. ABLE's agent library includes agents for prediction, classification, and clustering.[44] The ABLE programming framework is widely used and can be applied to a wide variety of applications, including autonomic computing; classification, clustering, and prediction in data-mining; diagnostics; planning; policy management; resource-balancing; and software management and installation.

General Electric
General Electric Transportation Systems has developed an AL capability for its locomotive engine business. This capability is enabled through an on-board computing and communications unit called LOCOCOMM®,[45] which hosts software applications and provides communications to General Electric's Monitoring and Diagnostics Service Center. Expert-on-Alert™ is one such software application that is designed to diagnose engine problems before they result in "road failures," i.e., locomotives that are stranded on the tracks away from maintenance facilities. The system continuously monitors locomotive parameters and transmits these data to a centralized database.

---

[42] Lin et al. (2002).

[43] Trebilcock (2004).

[44] Meyer (2004).

[45] See www.getransportation.com/general/locomotives/services/rm_d/lococomm.asp.

Automated diagnostics tools use rule-based techniques to screen the data for events that require maintenance intervention, and as trends are recognized in the data, the diagnostics tools are updated to reflect new system knowledge. Experienced maintainers at the service center review the repair recommendations, which are delivered automatically to the locomotive within 30 minutes of problem detection. The system then notifies the appropriate repair facility allowing for advance coordination of maintenance parts and labor. Smart Fueling® is another software application hosted on the LOCOCOMM unit. This application monitors each locomotive's location, fuel level, and consumption rate (both current and predicted) along with the dynamic fuel price at each fueling point, to create an optimized fueling plan that is updated hourly. In addition to the operational savings, reporting tools allow for the potential elimination of underused fuel depots, and increases in velocity are possible because of fewer fuel stops.

SAP

SAP presents itself as an "all-in-one" provider of the IT tools necessary for commercial companies to create adaptive supply chain networks (adaptive SCNs), which is its commercial interpretation of S&RL.[46] Adaptive SCNs are designed to be flexible, allowing for modifications in response to environmental changes while still achieving operational and financial efficiencies. Visibility of information across the supply chain (both intra- and interorganizationally) and velocity of response within the supply chain are presented as the preliminary conditions necessary for achievement of an adaptive SCN capability. Building on this foundation, adaptive SCNs exploit technology to interpret information in real time and use robust planning and execution capabilities to optimally respond to variations in the environment. The authors describe an available-to-promise (ATP) capability that receives a customer request, routes this request to all points in the supply chain that can fulfill the request (both inside and outside the organization), coordinates this information with the transportation planning across all providers, determines the optimal assignments autonomously, and

---

[46] See www.sap.com/solutions/business-suite/scm/pdf/50056466.pdf.

transmits this information back through the SCN all the way to the customer. These capabilities need to be sufficiently flexible to allow both for changes in customer orders and for replanning when monitoring systems detect supply chain disruptions. SAP presents the familiar set of technologies as adaptive SCN enablers: software agents, RFID, and Web services technology. The authors point out that agents are necessary for the continuous monitoring of vast amounts of data required to identify trends and proactively manage the SCN. The authors discuss the value added to firms through adaptive SCNs and posit the following:

- operational improvements to inventory turns, customer fill rates, capacity and labor use, obsolescence ratios, and service levels
- financial improvements with regard to free cash flow, cash-to-cash cycle times, and reduced working capital
- business performance ratio improvements to economic value added, return on assets, and return on invested capital.

This SAP white paper presents the adaptive SCN as an ultimate capability and does not provide any concrete examples or case studies of clients who have achieved this state. However, SAP claims that it can offer the entire suite of products necessary for this transition with robust integration technology.

General Motors OnStar®

OnStar is a General Motors service that currently involves primarily human communications and GPS tracking, but which is rapidly evolving into a probable harbinger of commercial AL, particularly with respect to prognostics and health monitoring for automobiles. The OnStar Safe & Sound® service includes functions such as accident detection and notification of airbag deployment, the contacting of emergency services, roadside assistance, remote car diagnostics, stolen vehicle tracking, accident assistance, personal calling, and a virtual advisor. Customers can reach OnStar manually or automatically at any time. Calls begin with the transfer of account information and location and then switch to voice. A human advisor assists with misadventures such as mechanical breakdown, car theft, or keys locked in the car. Via air bag deployment, OnStar can automatically detect an accident, and on newer models it can sense frontal, side, or rear impact without air bag deployment. Of greater interest to S&R applications are remote diagnostics that provide instant feedback on car trouble indicators, with the advisor providing information on their meaning and severity. If necessary, the advisor remotely queries car data for further interpretation, the vehicle transmits any problem codes and, using this information, the advisor recommends the required action. It is probable that the most fundamental prognostics and health monitoring, not requiring human involvement until an action is required, will be included in OnStar in the near future.

Robotics Institute—Carnegie Mellon University

The Intelligent Software Agents Lab at Carnegie Mellon University's Robotics Institute has developed RETSINA (Reusable Environment for Task-Structured Intelligent Networked Agents), an agent-based modeling infrastructure. Within this infrastructure, all agents are assumed to operate in a peer-to-peer environment, wherein no centralized coordination or control function exists to constrain the relations between agents. The RETSINA architecture is most applicable to the problem of communication coordination between diverse actors. A representative research project undertaken by the lab is "Information Fusion for Command and Control," a collaborative effort with other research institutions funded by the Air Force Office of Scientific Research. This effort addresses the increasing volume of information available to commanders through the development of a next-generation information system, which takes information feeds from various (and often conflicting) sources and autonomously creates a battlespace presentation useful to the commander. A software demonstration is presented at the project Web page,[47] in which an enemy biochemical weapons depot is detected, aerial reconnaissance provides confirmation of the target, and an air strike is executed against the target. Other research projects

---

[47] See www-2.cs.cmu.edu/~softagents/afosr_pret/demos.html (as of June 22, 2005).

at the lab include agent-based models for financial portfolio management and mobile communications networks.

Agent Technology Today and Tomorrow

In the foregoing description of S&R-related technologies, and our limited, but representative, look at research and development activities, issues, and programs, one may conclude that current and future success in implementing a full S&RCS capability is irrevocably tied to achieving current goals for agent-based systems. We reviewed many sources to form a coherent vision of the development and progress of this technology, its application areas, and likely barriers to adoption. The European Commission's Sixth Framework Program, AgentLink, created a roadmap to raise awareness and to promote adoption of agent technology.[48] We will highlight some of the major points of the AgentLink findings here. Table 3.1 shows the years in which the "main technologies" that can facilitate agent-based systems were developed. Depicted is the development of a vast array of middleware technologies supporting emerging enterprise-level systems. This technological infrastructure ranges from low-level wireless communication protocols such as Bluetooth to higher-level Web services technologies. Additionally, they also span the range of supported devices, from limited-capability devices such as mobile phones and PDAs to workstations and high-performance computers.

Some of the emerging trends identified by this group include Web services and grid computing; the drivers are ambient intelligence (interacting with other agents to achieve goals), autonomic computing, the semantic Web, and complex systems, all involving services that involve agents providing or consuming services. These trends and drivers say nothing specific about a whole range of specific areas within the field of agent-based computing, including human-agent interfaces, learning agents, robotic agents, and many others, but they provide a

---

[48] For more information, see Luck et al. (2005).

Table 3.1
Agent-Related Technologies for Infrastructure Support

Technology Type	Pre-1990	1990–1995	1995–2000	2000–2005
Internet technologies	email TCP IP	www HTTP	XML	SernWeb (OWL)
Remote procedure call		CORBA RMI		
Distributed object technologies			DCOM EJB	COM+ .NET
Peer-to-peer			(ICQ) instant messaging NAPSTER	Gnutella JXTA
Service-oriented technologies			Jini Java Spaces	UpaP
Pervasive computing			Bluetooth WiFi	
Web services				UDDI WSDL BPEL4WS SOAP
GRID				OGSA WSRF

context that is likely to drive forward the whole field. The AgentLink's conclusions validate our own assertion that research and development of agent technologies still has a long way to go. We have observed agent technologies in use in particular applications, but this is only the first wave of early adopters in sample contexts.

Without the proper metrics for measuring the agent (and other) technologies used in S&RCS implementation, it is difficult to project where or when CSC2 effectiveness best stands to gain from this technology insertion. We do believe that this is an important subject to address through IT prototyping for CSC2 because it should drive IT investments among S&RL technologies. The majority of experts believe that a medium-term vision and commitment of four to six years is likely for the development of relevant core technologies.[49]

Current multiagent systems are typically designed for a single corporate environment, with participating agents sharing common high-level goals in a single domain. These systems may be characterized as closed. The communications languages and interaction protocols are in-house, defined by design teams before agent interactions. Systems are usually scalable only under controlled, or simulated, conditions. Design approaches tend to be ad hoc, inspired by the agent paradigm rather than using any specific methodologies. Even if this is largely true, there is now an increased focus on, for example, taking methodologies out of the laboratory and into development environments, with commercial work being done to establish industrial-strength development techniques and notations. The work done in DARPA programs or by IBM's SAR Blue tends to be in this category. AgentLink's assessment is that, for the foreseeable future, there will be a substantial commercial demand for closed multiagent systems because of the security concerns that arise from open systems. Closed, well-protected systems are of equal or greater importance to military S&RCS applications.

The early results of this ongoing survey are that it is likely to be another six years before much general deployment of agent-based systems is seen. The mean expectation for mainstream deployment was the year 2011, with limited but identifiable deployment of agent technologies (such as negotiation) as part of eCommerce applications being achieved by 2007. In the general opinion of AgentLink's respondents, as well as our technology interviewees, even the above predictions are optimistic and much more research is needed. The majority of experts believed that a medium-term vision and commitment of four to six years was likely for the development of relevant core techniques, with a substantial number of respondents learning toward a longer-term timescale of seven to ten years.[50]

---

[49] Luck et al. (2004).

[50] Luck et al. (2004).

CHAPTER FOUR

Air Force CSC2 Implementation Effort

The Air Force has begun to take initial steps to implement the combat support command and control operational architecture. Its efforts are designed to help enable AEF operational goals. Implementation actions to date include changes in C2 doctrine, organizations, processes, and training. Although progress has been steady, the area of information systems and technology requires increasing application of modern capabilities. The emerging modernized logistics information systems emphasize mostly business process improvements, with little focus on CS challenges and requirements. Additionally, CS systems are not being coordinated and tested in an integrated way with operations and intelligence systems. The architecture and requirements for peacetime and wartime logistics and CS information systems will need to be more closely coordinated.

The Air Force has begun evaluating the effectiveness of CSC2 concepts in exercises. Improving CSC2 organizations; processes; and information systems hardware, software, and architecture will require several years of active involvement by USAF Headquarters and Air Force initiatives to restructure a system that was previously organized around fixed-base, fight-in-place air assets. However, there is active participation in structuring CSC2 activity and policy in a way that should effectively support forces throughout the 21st century. This chapter discusses Air Force CSC2 implementation actions.[1]

---

[1] For more information on RAND's analysis and recommendations, see Leftwich et al. (2002); Mills et al. (2006); Tripp. Lynch, et al. (2004); and Lynch et al. (2005).

Status of Implementation Actions

C2 Doctrine

The Air Force initiated a review of its doctrine and policy and began revisions to reflect the robust AEF CSC2 operational architecture. Changes are in the works to rewrite Air Force Doctrine Document (AFDD) 2-4. As AFDD-2, AFDD 2-6, and AFDD 2-8 come up for revision, they will also include CSC2 concepts. Further, Air Force policy and procedures are modified in Air Force Instructions (AFIs) and further explain the doctrinal concepts.[2] These actual and planned changes to Air Force doctrine and policy are on the right track. As doctrine is changed, procedures, policies, organizations, and systems can then be changed to align with the changing concepts of warfare. Perhaps the most significant opportunity for improvement is the integration of CS and operational planning. Currently, there are no standard processes for operational planners to communicate operational parameters to CS planners (e.g., beddown planning, TPFDD, planned ammunition expenditure rates, spares usage, transportation requirements). This deficiency greatly hinders timely, accurate CS planning. Early in the crisis action planning process, as planning responsibilities transition, CS planners often do not know operational requirements (with enough certainty to make CS plans). When operational parameters are supplied, they are often communicated inconsistently to CS planners.[3] Creating a framework, reinforced in doctrine, to delineate specifically what information operations planners provide, in what format, and to whom could address this shortfall. Solidifying this linkage between operations and logistics in crisis

---

[2]   Sullivan (2003).

[3]   Apparently, during Operation Iraqi Freedom (OIF) planning, USAFE ammunitions planners were able to get good information ("90 percent") as early as September 2002 to make their plans (USAFE/LGMW). Others were not. For example, AFMC/LSO, which had to make transportation cost projections for deployment and sustainment, and were forced to use best guesses based on little real information (personal communication with Mr. Howard English, AFMC/LSO). USAFE fuels planners also reported general problems getting operational requirement data (personal communication with SMSgt Howard Heisey, USAFE/LGSF).

action planning would enable a step forward in the coordination, timeliness, and accuracy of CS planning.

Organizations and Processes

The Air Force has made progress in

- establishing standing CS organizations with clear C2 responsibilities
- developing processes and procedures for centralized management of CS support resources and capabilities.

The Air Force's proposed CSC2 nodal construct, which is consistent with its CSC2 operational architecture, required that the alignment of command and control responsibilities be clearly defined and assigned to standard CS nodes and has made plans to designate specific organizations to fulfill the responsibilities of each node. Actions have already been taken to move in this direction. Although some organizational developments were inspired by the architecture and associated analysis, other developments, corresponding to concepts in the AEF CSC2 operational architecture, have occurred in response to the demands of recent operations.

Operations Support Centers

Operations Support Centers (OSCs) are examples of continuously developing organizational nodes that correspond to modern CSC2 architectural concepts. Within several MAJCOMs, OSCs have evolved as a matter of necessity for handling the day-to-day operations that did not fall under their Title X "organize, train, and equip" responsibilities but were too great for a Numbered Air Force (NAF) to manage alone.[4] Air Combat Command (ACC), USAFE, and the Pacific Air Force (PACAF) each have their own OSC developed in response to real world demands.[5] During recent contingencies, they have served many

---

[4] Sullivan (2003).

[5] These are at various stages of evolution and each MAJCOM has its own label for an OSC: In USAFE, it is called the USAFE Theater Air Support Center (UTASC) and in PACAF, it is called the PACAF OSC (POSC). ACC is currently forming an OSC.

important functions. These correctly positioned and manned C2 nodes are a critical piece in aligning C2 responsibilities in peacetime that will continue unchanged during contingencies and conflict.

Commodity Control Points

CCPs already exist within organizations that manage Air Force resources. The CSC2 architecture requires continual enhancements to the CCPs. During Operation Enduring Freedom (OEF), AFMC/ LG assumed many of the responsibilities identified with a spares CCP, such as tracking spares shipments end-to-end, forecasting demands, and working more closely with customers and suppliers. AFMC also drafted a concept of operation (CONOP) for a spares CCP with features like those required in a modern CSC2 architecture.[6] Learning from past experiences, AFMC established the Warfighter Sustainment Division to specifically address problems with wartime combat support. The Warfighter Sustainment Division, consisting of an Operations Branch and a Logistics Analysis Branch, was created to be a single interface between AFMC and its warfighting customers.

Combat Support Center

At the Air Force level, the operational architecture calls for the CSC to monitor CS requests for a particular contingency and assess the effects of those requests on the ability to support that and other contingencies. During OEF, the existing Air Force CSC assumed many responsibilities of future CSC2 such as integrating multitheater requirements, identifying global resource constraints by commodity, conducting integrated assessments (base support), and recommending allocation actions for critical resources. The CSC performed these functions and intervened when necessary to allocate scarce resources to the AOR when those resources might have been designated to support other AORs and other potential contingencies. In OEF, the CSC did the worldwide assessment of FOL support capability, determined when the Air Force could provide support for other services, and made recommendations to the Joint Chiefs of Staff accordingly. The Air Force Agile Combat

---

[6]   Headquarters, Air Force Materiel Command (2003).

Execution Support (ACES) team performed the functions of the CSC for OIF. In addition to conducting integrated assessments, such as base support, the ACES team tracked and monitored many action items identified in the Logistics Supportability Analysis (LSA) and worked to find solutions to the competing demands of scarce resources. The ACES team took a global view of CS and, while working for the A4/7 (formerly AF/IL), was able to cross MAJCOMs and theaters to find optimal solutions.[7] This is precisely the kind of well informed, empowered CSC organizations that will be necessary at all levels to sense and respond to conditions on the modern battlefield.

Training

The Air Force has made much progress in improving CSC2 training. An Education Working Group has been formed to address the development and enhancement of formal education programs. The Air Force Advanced Maintenance and Munitions Officers School at Nellis Air Force Base, Nevada, has implemented significant C2 instruction in its curriculum.[8] ACS is now part of a "Logistics of Waging War" course at the Air Force Academy. The Support Group Commanders Course and the new CS Executive Warrior Program will provide training for Support Group commanders, who are potential expeditionary Support Group commanders and A-4s. On the academic side, one of the Air Command and Staff College's eight new specialized studies provides an overview of ACS for officers and civilians within and outside the ACS community. The Air Force Institute of Technology (AFIT) is revamping short courses to align with the new combat wing organization and logistics processes. Finally, the Advanced Logistics Readiness Officer Course will provide logistics expertise to the warfighter.

Information Systems

This area needs the most change. These changes should include the following:

---

[7] Tripp et al. (2004).

[8] Sullivan (2003).

- Relate operational plans to CS requirements.
- Convert CS resource levels to operational capabilities.
- Conduct capability assessment and aggregate on a theater or global scale.
- Conduct tradeoff analyses of operational, support, and strategy options.
- Focus integration efforts on global implementation of a few selected tools.
- Standardize tools and systems for consistent integration.

Joint Flow and Sustainment Transportation (JFAST), developed under and managed by USTRANSCOM, is an automated system that tests the transportation feasibility of executable TPFDDs. This is an example of the beginnings of the new kind of system required for modern CSC2. These systems will need to include the following common features:

- linkage of CS performance data to operational requirements
- transformation of data into actionable processed information
- simplicity and accuracy
- real-time assessment and automated analysis capability.

Most of the logistics information systems' modernization efforts revolve around improving databasing (moving to Web-based technologies) and developing a common operating picture, which will give asset visibility to users throughout the CS network. The accuracy and availability of data should improve with these modernization efforts.

However, most of the modernization is linked to improving information technology solutions, which support day-to-day business processes. Modernization of the peacetime systems will certainly yield some improved CSC2 information ability. However, the requirements for a more robust S&RCS capability need to be considered within the wartime CSC2 architecture. Combat support system modernization will need to assess both peacetime and deployment requirements and produce tools and capabilities that will satisfy business processes as well as CSC2 needs.

The Air Force has created an implementation team to begin these essential changes to information systems. It will be the team's charge to take the operational architecture; solicit comments from Air Force Component Commands, Air Staff, and MAJCOMs; and integrate lessons learned from previous and ongoing operations to develop and refine an executable implementation plan.

The Air Force already has some tools that perform a subset of the recommended functions. The following are representative examples:

- The EXPRESS Planning Module (EPM) tool can predict customer needs, prioritize them, and evaluate depot resource availability.
- The Advanced Planning and Scheduling COTS tool has capabilities similar to those of EPM.
- The FMSE calculator is a Microsoft® Excel®-based tool created at the Air Force Petroleum (AFPET) office that translates operational parameters (e.g., aircraft type, sorties) into CS requirements (e.g., UTCs). It is under continuous development but has already been used for execution by fuels planners. This is another example of the kind of tools that will enable the TO-BE CSC2 vision to become a reality.

Another information system capability that must be developed to support the AEF CSC2 architecture is one in which working-level CS personnel can input resource and process information that then automatically generates capability assessments for higher-level visibility. Some munitions and petroleum, oils, and lubricants (POL) reports already do this well. PACAF has Web-based munitions and POL reports that are generated automatically in several formats for various organizational-level–appropriate CS leaders. This is the kind of information system function necessary to enable an S&RCS capability within the CSC2 system.

Enterprise-Wide Systems and Combat Support Command and Control

The Air Force has begun to modernize information systems, not only in logistics but also in virtually every category of support and operations. It is recognized that enterprise resource planning (ERP) systems are needed to replace old, stovepiped systems. An ERP system includes hardware and software that manages an organization's transactional data on a continuous, real-time basis. An ERP system would standardize the data and information systems for supply, maintenance, logistics, and many other CS functions across multiple locations.[9] Enterprise architecture views are currently being developed for improved logistics business processes. As these are being developed, however, it is important that derivative architecture views be developed that will clarify and enhance warfighting C2 needs as well. For the ERP solutions to support warfighter C2 needs, they must be shaped to be equally effective at facilitating and reporting continuous business processes and management information requirements as well as at automatically feeding appropriate information into CSC2 analytical tools and presentation layers in a near-real-time mode. In the same way that new weapon capabilities have resulted in increased operational effects, new IT technologies facilitate the possibility of improved management of logistics assets. Net-centric information activity allows the CSC2 warfighters to match operational decisionmaking rates and efficacy.

CSC2 analytical and presentation tools will need to augment typical data-processing with increasingly modern S&R capabilities. Batch processing and analysis, a proven rate and methodology for most of the Air Force's 60 years of experience, will not effectively support agile combat operations and effects-based metrics. To respond to continuously changing desired effects, enemy actions, rates of consumption, and other controlling inputs, the 21st century logistics warfighter will need to accumulate, correlate, and display information rapidly and in graphic formats that will be equally understandable for operators and

---

[9]   For further discussion of ERP systems and their effect on supply chain management, see Bowersox, Closs, and Hall (1998).

logisticians. Data will need to be refreshed much more rapidly than the former monthly and quarterly cycles. Daily decisions will require daily (if not hourly or possibly continuous) data refresh cycles.

Closed-Loop Planning and Control Systems

A closed-loop planning and control system is essential to a robust military S&RCS architecture. EPM and APS, described above, are two systems that may meet architectural requirements for closed-loop spares planning. Currently, information about Air Force resource and process metrics is organized by commodity or end item and located on disparate information systems. Creating a single system accessible to a wide audience would enhance leadership visibility over these resources. Such a system needs to have enough automation to translate lower-level process and data into aggregated metrics, which can be related in most cases to operational requirements.

Current development and testing of closed-loop planning and control systems has not been well coordinated with parallel efforts in the operations and intelligence communities. Although information technology improvements supporting peacetime business processes can be developed without operations coordination, CSC2 systems will need to be increasingly coordinated and tested in conjunction with operations and intelligence suites of systems and tools. Currently, the Air Force Command and Control Intelligence, Surveillance and Reconnaissance Center (AFC2ISRC) is tasked with developing and testing C2 tools. The AFC2ISRC has an A4 (logistics) staff element that could exercise responsibility for developing CSC2 tools under the AFC2ISRC charter. This role would need to be supported by the AFC2ISRC/CC and the Air Force Deputy Chief of Staff for Installations and Logistics (A4/7, formerly AF/IL) and the AFC2ISRC mission statement might be necessary to emphasize the importance of the CSC2 development responsibility. Staffing levels to accomplish the new responsibilities may need to be reviewed to ensure that they are adequate to handle the added responsibilities.

To develop effective CSC2 tools that accurately link logistics levels and rates to operational effects, modern CSC2 tools must be developed and tested in conjunction with operations and intelligence systems.

Although the logistics community works to eliminate the stove-piped systems within its community, it must also work at the integration of logistics information with other users outside the traditional logistics community. The AFC2ISRC is a logical venue for the development and testing of all CSC2 capabilities that support warfighting nodes to ensure that CS modernization tools and methods work in conjunction with those emerging within the operations community.

Rapid deployment and capabilities-based planning have been emphasized in our description of the TO-BE architecture. Having a rapid, flexible deployment process suggests the need for a rapid TPFDD planning tool. RAND analysis has recently produced a prototype of a requirements generator.[10] A fully developed version of this tool could enable the kind of quick planning prescribed by an AEF-driven CSC2 operational architecture.

The greatest change required in modernized logistics systems is to reorient existing logistics systems toward combat-oriented ones. The peacetime-only materiel management systems need to be structured to participate in the enterprise-wide sharing of data and culling of information. Stand-alone, single-function systems need to be replaced with systems that serve several functions for CS leaders at all echelons and modern CSC2 systems need to provide information useful in both peacetime and wartime decisionmaking.

CSC2 Concepts Are Being Evaluated in Exercises
The Air Force is using joint-services high-level logistics wargames (e.g., Future Logistics Wargame [FLOW]) to evaluate new concepts. Tactical-level exercises (e.g., Silver Flag) are being used to expand CS skills training. Eagle Flag, another exercise designed for the CS personnel responsible for opening and establishing deployed bare bases, gives personnel the final field training exercise before their AEF rotation and gives them an opportunity to test their ability to open and establish an airbase and provide effective CSC2. As the Air Force begins to transition to the AEF CSC2 operational architecture, the Directorate of Readiness (A4R, formerly AF/ILG) has been tasked to assess the imple-

[10] Snyder and Mills (2004).

mentation effectiveness. First was to observe the steps toward a robust CSC2 capability in an operational environment. Terminal Fury 2004 (TF 04), an annual Pacific Command (PACOM) exercise, provided an opportunity to observe important CSC2 nodes in an operational environment. TF 04 was used to assess the CSC2 nodes and information flows in the modern CSC2 operational architecture to explore and build knowledge about integrated CS systems and processes. The exercise offered the opportunity to observe a number of CSC2 nodes involved in the exercise scenario including the Joint Forces Air Component Commander (JFACC), the Joint Air Operations Center (JAOC) Forward, the Air Operations Center Rear, the Air Force Forces Forward (which is the assigned Numbered Air Force 13 AF), and the AFFOR Rear (the PACAF OSC). Personnel at the Air Force CSC, AFMC, the Air Mobility Command, and the AFC2ISRC were asked to investigate potential effects on these Air Force–unique nodes. The goal was to observe the existing CSC2 node processes and architecture as they interact with the TF 04 exercise environment, making observations about the activity and assessing movement toward AEF CSC2 architecture. The exercise also highlighted that S&CS capabilities are nearly non-existent and that logisticians today, at the various nodes, must use expert judgment to address logistics issues in terms of operationally relevant metrics or leave the questions begging. Future C2 exercises will increasingly incorporate and test CSC2 effectiveness and look for opportunities to enhance integration and sharing of information systems.

Future Work to Implement TO-BE CSC2 Operational Architecture

The Air Force plans call for the CSC2 implementation effort to be fully integrated with the expeditionary logistics concept (eLOG21),[11] Global Combat Support System (GCCS), and other CS enterprise architectures. Systems and technical architecture views compliant with the Enterprise Architecture Initiative are to be developed. The CSC2 tools that provide responsive capability analysis, wartime and contingency

---

[11] eLog21 is the Air Force transformation campaign plan to improve logistics to meet both the current and future threat environment (see U.S. Air Force, 2002a).

decision support for the resource arbitration process, CS execution feedback, and forward-looking assessments will need to reside within the systems architecture. These tools should strengthen communication channels between supporting and supported functions. A4I (formerly AF/ILI) and A4RX (formerly AF/ILGX) will work together to integrate CSC2 architectures and the Future Logistics Enterprise to build the foundation for making combat support truly agile.[12] The Air Force has made much progress in implementing doctrine and policy changes to effect procedural and system changes to the AEF CSC2 architecture. There are still gaps between requirements and capabilities in developing and testing information technology solutions and architectures, but plans are in place to continue to close these gaps.

---

[12] Sullivan (2003).

CHAPTER FIVE

Future Work and Challenges

The Air Force has made some progress in implementing doctrine and policy changes, and plans are in place to continue to close the information technology and analytical tools gaps. An expanded Air Force TO-BE CSC2 execution planning and control architecture system would enable the Air Force to meet its AEF operational goals. New capabilities include the following:

- Enable the CS community to quickly estimate support requirements for force package options and assess the feasibility of operational and support plans.
- Facilitate quick determination of beddown needs and capabilities.
- Ensure rapid TPFDD development.
- Support development and configuration of theater distribution networks to meet Air Force employment timelines and resupply needs.
- Facilitate the development of resupply plans and monitor performance.
- Determine the effects of allocating scarce resources to various combatant commanders.
- Indicate when CS performance begins to deviate from desired states and facilitate development and implementation of get-well plans.

Dynamic Feedback—The Foundation for S&RCS

Combat support and operations activities must be continuously monitored for changes in performance and regulated to keep within planned objectives. Today, in-theater asset visibility is limited, whereas in-transit visibility is improving. CS feedback data such as resource levels, rates of consumption, critical component removal rates, and critical process performance times such as repair times, munitions build-up times, in-transit times, infrastructure capacity, and site-preparation times will be the focus of attention for S&R systems. Because operations can change suddenly, these data must be continuously available throughout operations to make needed adjustments. New CSC2 systems will need to be better coordinated with operations and intelligence systems. In the developmental stages, data structuring and sharing methodologies will need to be coordinated with the rest of the Air Force C2 architecture. When monitoring reveals a mismatch between desired and actual resource, or process performance levels, intervention at the various levels of CSC2 nodes will be initiated. Discrepancies between desired and actual levels of support may arise from changes in CS performance or in operations. Assessment must be able to quickly address CS performance problems or changes and estimate CS requirements to meet changing operational objectives.[1]

Significant advances must be made in the way planning, directing, coordinating, and controlling functions are performed to move the Air Force toward a robust S&RCS capability. These essential elements of an effective C2 system must be altered to allow them to accomplish the important aspects of sensing and responding to changes in operating parameters when the violation of tolerance becomes evident. These S&R activities will need to take place in a nearly real-time environment. The objective of rapid sensing and response is to alert decisionmakers to initial deviations in the plan, rather than reacting, after the fact, to situations affecting mission capability. Emphases of metrics in the future need to be on "outcomes," rather than on "outputs."

---

[1]   Leftwich et al. (2002).

Necessary adaptations include at the minimum the following improvements in CSC2 architecture and activities.

Planning

With the AEF's short timelines and pipelines, it is critical to be able to add CS information to initial planning, giving planners flexibility and confidence. CS execution planning functions include monitoring theater and global CS resource levels and process performance, estimating resource needs for a dynamic and changing campaign, and assessing plan feasibility. Because capabilities and requirements are constantly changing, these activities must be performed continuously so that accurate data are available for courses of action and ongoing ad hoc operational planning. Planning also includes assessment and ongoing monitoring of CS infrastructure configurations (FOLs, FSLs, CONUS support locations, theater distribution systems, C2 nodes) that support the operations plan. Benefits and drawbacks of various support options (use of FSLs, sources of supply, transportation providers, modes and nodes, host nation support) must be weighed in the context of timelines, operational capability, support risk, and cost. Having complete, up-to-date information on FOL capacities and operational capabilities and their support allows more CS information to play in early planning stages (such as COA development). CS execution planning should result in the production of a logistically feasible operations plan—one that dictates infrastructure configuration, a C2 organization structure, a TDS, and CS resource and process control metrics.

The first step in planning is to estimate CS resource needs based on the operational requirements, which are typically defined in terms of required sorties by weapon system type. Care must be taken to incorporate uncertainty and potential actions by the adversary into the planning process. Given an uncertain set of operational scenarios and strategic goals, an agile, robust CS system for execution planning and control should be able to meet a wide range of potential outcomes.

Support planners need to know U.S. capabilities at both the theater and global levels, which requires centralized CS information to track each commodity resource level and support tools and trained personnel to aggregate the resource reports and convert them to operational capability measures. With the capability measures, CS personnel can assess the feasibility and implications of each operational and support option and present a trade space of feasible support options to operational planners. With this trade space, the planners can select a strategy, fully understanding its support implications, and can determine how the CS network should be tailored to best fit the chosen scenario. This is essential to developing an effects-based operational plan.

Combat support infrastructure tailoring actions can take many forms. Configuration actions can address the use of CIRFs, development of the distribution network, or the identification of sources of supply (SOSs), to name just a few. The support plan should establish inventory levels for such commodities as spare parts, munitions, and fuel, including safety stocks, at each node of the CS infrastructure, and it should protect against uncertainty. Other elements of the CS plan include the expected performance of the CS infrastructure and the expected consumption of resources based on the planned operational tempo. Planning factors include parking capacity of aircraft ramps, potential fuel consumption versus available fuel storage, critical water and power capacities, expected removal rates for repairables, expected repair times for commodities through the various repair facilities, expected response times at various points within the distribution network, and expected munitions expenditure rates. These planning factors become critical inputs to the decision support tools that provide the "look ahead" capability that enables CS to be proactive.[2] Increasingly, information like this will need to feed automatically into operations and intelligence C2 systems. Certain information will likewise need to feed automatically into the CSC2 tools. Modern C2

---

[2] Recently, 7th Air Force planners developed a modeling capability, using an Air Force model called THUNDER, to determine the effect of critical munitions availability on their war plan. This capability is a positive step for incorporating CS modeling into operations plans, as discussed above. In their assessments, 7th Air Force planners will examine how reallocation of smart munitions from the Korean AOR to the air war over Afghanistan will affect movement of the Forward Edge of the Battle Area and additional aircraft and sorties that might be needed to compensate for the lower effectiveness of fewer smart bombs used against targets. They then will explore bedding down the additional aircraft on the Korean Peninsula.

systems will need to have fewer interfaces and passing of reformatted data. Portions of the CS and operations databases will need to be viewable by operators and logisticians. Compartmentalized, stove-piped systems will need to be modernized with net-centric-capable data and analytical tools.

The support network is configured from initial plans. Most configuration takes place at the start of the execution phase, although some preparation of the battlefield for contingencies is carried out during strategic planning. Consolidating beddown of like aircraft types, resourcing theater distribution assets, prepositioning WRM, creating standing centralized maintenance facilities, or establishing C2 nodes are just a few examples of strategic configuration. The next step is to assess the capability of the configured infrastructure. Staffs need to determine whether airfield capacity (ramp, fuel, munitions, power, and water), inventories, supply sources, repair facilities, and the distribution network can support operational requirements. Anticipated shortfalls will require retailoring of the infrastructure configuration plan.

The plan will be assessed against a set of metrics tied to goals such as sortie production capability. If no feasible CS plan can be created within reasonable cost, CS leaders must provide alternatives, presenting the tradeoffs between CS resources required and operational performance achieved. The plan-assess-replan iterations continue until an acceptable solution is found.[3] The final step is to define any further configuration actions as the plan is executed. As mentioned above, configuration actions in the support plan are expected to take into account the dynamic nature of operational requirements and the resources needed to mitigate the risk of variability in forecasted demands and in the CS processes.

Directing

CS directing activities include configuring and tailoring the CS network and establishing process performance parameters and resource

---

[3] The 7th Air Force munitions example in the preceding footnote provides insight into the type of assessments required here. We note that this type of assessment is needed for contingencies and unplanned wars and is not limited to canonical planning scenarios.

thresholds.[4] Planning output drives infrastructure configuration direction—there must be an ongoing awareness of CS infrastructure and transportation capabilities to feed into operational planning and execution. For example, the speed and precision with which beddown sites can be assessed and prepared (configured) improve with the amount of information available beforehand. Knowing the precise configuration for various options, in turn, gives planners more speed and flexibility in the employment of forces in the face of changing objectives or constraints. The ability to reconfigure the support infrastructure quickly enables operational changes, be they the result of anticipated or unanticipated changes in a scenario. Timely, accurate information and an agile CS system able to execute network configuration decisions would thus allow leaders to respond more quickly, or simply to make more informed decisions. Along similar lines, identifying and using appropriate sources (e.g., ships, supply depots, or host nation contractors) for different commodities (e.g., ammunition, fuel, or spares) and required services (construction, billeting, feeding) allow maximum employment of available Air Force and joint-service resources and the opportunity to balance intra- and intertheater requirements to support all AORs. As operational objectives change, requiring different logistics or installation support, the source can be changed. Also, as operational locations change, the source, as part of the overall CS network, can change to meet the demands more quickly.

Once combat operations commence, the logistics and installations support infrastructure must be regulated to ensure continued support for dynamic operations. The system must monitor actual CS performance against the plan. The performance parameters and resource buffers established during execution planning will provide advance warning of potential system failure. In the increasingly complex world of expeditionary operations, more of the data accumulation, analysis, and presentation will need to be accomplished automatically. This is an area in which agent-based analysis and alerting will be extremely valuable. As the amount and complexity of the data increase, C2 leader-

---

[4] Heuristically determined thresholds can be established while more sophisticated expert rules or algorithms are being developed. For instance, Brigadier General Hennessey (AMC/

ship in-theater will need improved analytical tools to help them determine the best possible replan and redistribution options. When CS performance diverges from the desired level, the system must be able to detect the change and proactively modify the original plan, develop a get-well plan, and reassess the modified plan's feasibility. Plan feasibility needs to be assessed continuously. Safety measures, inventories, and high-level metrics are key elements in CS monitoring and control.[5] Emerging information system technologies offer the promise of faster, more informed option analysis. Response will be increasingly focused on emerging conditions or rates, rather than on work stoppages and out-of-stock occurrences. The "directing," "coordinating," and "controlling" phases are those in which sensing and responding to moment-by-moment changes will be important.

Coordinating

Coordination ensures a common operating picture for CS personnel. It includes beddown site status, weapon system availability, sortie production capabilities, and the like. Coordination activities should be geared to providing information to higher headquarters, not necessarily to seek a decision but to create an advance awareness of issues should one be needed at a later date. Great effort must be made to effectively filter the information flows up the command chain, to avoid overwhelming commanders with information of little utility, but to provide sufficient information to improve battlespace awareness. CS coordination tasks will affect theater distribution, force closure, supply deployment, and allocation of support forces. Each of these activities requires information gathered from a variety of processes and organizations to be consolidated into a single decisionmaking framework that delivers decision-quality data to planners and commanders. For example, to coordinate TDS movements, CS personnel must monitor

---

LG) uses zero-balance stock positions coupled with forces supporting an engaged combatant commander as a rule to determine when lateral actions should be taken to resupply a unit "at war." Using this rule, he authorizes the AMC/Regional Supply Squadron (RSS) to reallocate stocks from units with stock to those with zero balances. The idea is to prevent mission degradation by focusing attention on the items that will cause the next mission degradation.

[5] Leftwich et al. (2002).

all parts of the theater, as well as the activities of USTRANSCOM, other U.S. military services, coalition partners, and host nations. Information technology solutions to CSC2 requirements will need to include the ability to share information with these partners and to view data from their systems. Similarly, base-level planning usually depends on supplies provided by intratheater distribution. To develop supportable plans, operational and support planners must understand what the TDS will provide at any given time. Policy should specify the information to be collected and dictate how it should be gathered and disseminated to organizations for both decisionmaking and for maintaining situational awareness.

Controlling

During the execution of peacetime and contingency operations, CS control tracks CS activities, resource inventories, and process performance worldwide, assessing root causes when performance deteriorates, deviates from what is expected, or otherwise falls out of control. Control modifies the CS infrastructure to return CS performance to the desired state. CS control should evaluate the feasibility of proposed modifications before they are implemented and then direct the appropriate organizations to implement the changes. Although doctrine must define and establish CS execution planning and control functions and objectives as described above, it should also prescribe which organizations perform these functions. Doctrine should delineate the roles and responsibilities of directorates within the AFFOR, divisions of the AOC, and other support organizations. It should include the reporting hierarchy and the communications network between groups. Once the "what" and "who" are delineated in doctrine, AFIs should detail "how" the function will be executed by describing tasks performed by each organization, the information that each group should consider in its decisionmaking, where that data stream will come from, and how frequently this information is updated. Presentation tools will need to become increasingly standardized with options for tailoring to meet specific theater requirements. Elevating the importance of CS execution planning and control in Air Force doctrine can engender enforceable rules for each organization, document information to be shared, and enable a much-improved planning process.[6]

Information Systems and Decision Support Tools

Key to achieving an effective S&RCS capability is the complete modernization of CS communication networks and systems software. Many of the current systems tabulate data but do little to analyze and process those data into actionable information or to recommended alternatives. Most analysis occurs after the fact. Data are gathered and then analyzed. Modern systems will need to respond to changes in rates, which are measured in real time. Current maintenance and supply information systems will need to be increasingly fashioned to become network-wide decision support tools. Information will need to be networked more, so that decisionmakers at every level see the same information set in near real time. For several reasons, existing systems cannot support these requirements,[7] primarily because of the lack of uniformity among systems. Because CS resources have been managed by stove-pipes and funded by commodity, with different organizations having commodity management responsibility, corresponding information systems have been developed and implemented independently in the organizations. The result is a myriad of independent systems with little ability to share data or interface with other systems.[8] Thus, although these systems allow individual commodity data to be recorded and monitored, they do not facilitate the integration of the data for comprehensive CS resource monitoring and capability assessments. Furthermore, with such a proliferation of systems, data in each are updated only

---

[6] Leftwich et al. (2002).

[7] Personal communication with Lt Col Stephen Luxion, HQ CENTAF A-3/A-5, February 8, 2001; HQ AFMC LGXX, February 21, 2001; Mr. Van Hazel, 7th Air Force operations research analyst, December 10, 2001; Major Parker Northrup, 7th Air Force Air Operations Group, December 10, 2001; Major Steen, PACAF/XPXX, December 17, 2001; and Lt Col Levault, 13th AF/A3/5, December 13, 2001.

[8] Headquarters, CENTAF (2001a).

sporadically,[9] and update status and data reliability are often unknown to users. Existing information systems also lack robustness. Reliable recording of time-sensitive and often classified data within a globally distributed mobile organization like the Air Force is inherently challenging.[10] For example, logistics planning factors, which govern the translation of operational plans to CS resource requirements, are updated only every few years.[11] Similarly, base/host nation infrastructure capacity is updated only on an as-needed or contingency-driven basis.[12] These factors result in CS plans that are not reliable. In addition, CS planners may not be aware of tools available to estimate CS requirements.[13] The C2 tools to support CS transformation will need to be altered significantly. The AEF transformation requires equally transformation of C2 systems and architecture. Highly mobile, rapid-reactive AEF forces will not be able to respond rapidly to the changing battlefield CS situation using the management-oriented CSC2 systems designed for another, more predictable era.

New Sense and Respond Systems

Systems are needed that will constantly monitor CS capacity, resource inventory, and process performance levels. Tools are needed to convert operational plans and status information into CS resource requirements and resource levels and then into operational capabilities. Tools are also needed to inform maintenance workload decisions by expressing infrastructure status in terms of operational capabilities and estimating resupply, beddown, and associated sustainment requirements. These tools will enable the Air Force to more accurately express its

---

[9]   Headquarters, Joint Chiefs of Staff (2001).

[10]   Headquarters, Air Force Materiel Command (2001).

[11]   Headquarters, CENTAF A-4 (2001b).

[12]   Headquarters, CENTAF A-7 (2002).

[13]   In the Air War Over Serbia (AWOS), USAFE CS planners were not aware of LOGSAFE, a tool to estimate resupply transportation requirements. See Feinberg et al. (2001). During the early months of OEF, Air Mobility Command (AMC) CS planners were unaware of ACC and PACAF GeoReach remote base imaging and mapping capability. For more information, see Leftwich et al (2002).

resupply and sustainment needs. Finally, tools are needed to aid bed-down decisions. Some of these requirements can be supported by integrating and modifying existing systems, whereas others will require new system development.

A thorough evaluation should consider all decision support tools for a particular function, with implementation focused on a smaller set of tools worldwide. This will reduce the number of systems and training programs required for each planning function and will permit an efficient transfer of information. New analytical and presentation tools should be built on a systems infrastructure that can rapidly transfer information to maintenance facilities, inventory control points, AFFOR staff, and other key CS nodes, as well as the AOC and all relevant operational nodes. This infrastructure will maximize the productivity of new tools and allow them to interface with joint-service systems. Air Force actions can then be framed in the context of a joint-service campaign with information disseminated on a timely basis. The effects of improved information systems and decision support tools will be felt throughout the TO-BE process. Properly integrating information from these tools will greatly reduce the chances of needing to revise a plan in midstream because of unforeseen CS constraints, allow a faster transition to war and better-informed decisions, and facilitate change when necessary.

Enhancement of information systems and decision support tools is a challenging and difficult task in any organization, but it is particularly challenging in the Air Force CS area because of the new C2 functions that need to be supported. The value of each additional capability will need to be considered as well as its cost. The Air Force may consider seeking external advice on how to best address this issue. The RAND architecture provides a view of the processes and functions that must be developed to better develop CS planning and execution responsibilities across the spectrum of operations.

Agents and Related Technology

Some of the military research and development initiatives have adopted agent-based computing and other S&RL technology applications as part of their efforts to incorporate S&RL concepts. However, some detractors of S&RL development view it as a system that can be incorporated or adopted by other systems such as Global Combat Support System.[14] As we pointed out above, S&RL, and its broader definition, S&RCS, is not system architecture, a system of systems, a group of applications or functional domains, or a data warehouse. It is a way to manage actionable information and coordinate decisionmaking and to do it more effectively by applying specific technologies. There are many alternatives for integrating S&RL technologies, provided that the concept retains the focus described throughout this report. GCSS, which is a DoD-wide enterprise, may share many, but not all, common S&RL requirements; however, it does not address the need to begin S&RL technology insertion into each service's information technology and weapon systems programs today. GCSS may well be another applicable prototype for the integration of S&RL technologies, but it is an inappropriate advocacy and management vehicle for co-evolution of the concept across DoD programs.

We note that an effort is being made by DoD to establish networks of practitioners and researchers with common interests from academia, R&D labs, industry and commerce, and military organizations and to organize meetings on specific topics to enable the sharing of knowledge and experience. Disseminating this information widely through Internet sites and by frequent updates to OFT's S&RL documents in a timely fashion may require more emphasis within OSD Acquisition, Technology, and Logistics (AT&L) or where the responsibility rests for such dissemination. At the DoD level, stimulating and funding research on problems of critical importance to the deployment of agent systems in the emerging computer environments, as with other technologies for S&RL realization, must be actively pursued.

At present, there is continuing development of the information technology base necessary to enable a more rapid and accurate responding logistics via S&RCS technology insertion. Operation Iraqi Freedom

---

[14] Some argue that the baseline system for meeting DoD's network-centric as well as the S&RL requirements should be GCSS, projecting it to be fully operational in 2006. They recommend that OFT's S&RL development team terminate its efforts and that OFT's S&RL requirements and program be consolidated into GCSS (see Newkirk and Currie, 2005).

highlighted the need for a better S&R capability while demonstrating how adoption of some of the key elements of S&RL concepts, such as network centric warfare and more adaptive combat systems, contributed to many of the combat successes.[15]

The dynamic organizational learning and change prescribed by commercial S&R paradigms and described by computational organization science through agent-based modeling could present a fundamental challenge to Air Force chain-of-command doctrine. However, because ABMs are able to model authority and communication structures within an organization, a well-specified model would permit the Air Force to explore the effectiveness and robustness of alternative policies, such as lateral support, for supply chain management, authority, and communications.

Finally, ABMs can be used to test intelligent multi-agent systems before they are brought online in commercial or military settings, by including agents that represent humans interacting with the SCM systems.

Toward a Responsive System

The strategic and operational environment and the AEF concept that addresses it present significant challenges to the current CS structure. The Air Force has taken solid steps toward addressing these challenges by creating and beginning the implementation of a CSC2 operational architecture. Adapting remaining deficiencies in CS execution planning and control is integral to the continued success of this effort. The CSC2 system of the future must have the S&RCS capabilities needed to be able to continuously monitor CS resource levels and translate them into operational metrics, evaluating the resources needed to achieve operational goals, assessing the feasibility of support options, and helping to develop alternative plans. It must rapidly reconfigure the CS infrastructure to meet specific contingency scenario needs and proactively preempt operational compromises that result because of CS

---

[15] Science Applications International Corporation (n.d.), p. 12.

constraints through the use of commodity and process control metrics and process monitoring to regulate support processes. Such a CSC2 system requires S&RCS capabilities to meet its goal of adjusting support activities during execution to optimize warfighter support. The CSC2 TO-BE operational configuration must be designed around a highly informed, responsive CS community able to flawlessly plan, execute, and sustain support of both the peacetime operations and the highly unpredictable contingency and wartime operations of the future.

Significant challenges remain before the Air Force can realize an S&RCS capability. To develop effective CSC2 tools that accurately link logistics levels and rates to operational effects, modern CSC2 tools must be developed and tested in conjunction with operations and intelligence systems. However, as noted above, the AFC2ISRC is responsible for the development and testing of all C2 tools *except* for logistics tools. Only through integrated testing can the CSC2 architecture be properly developed and implemented. The AFC2ISRC has an A4 (logistics) staff element that could exercise responsibility for developing and leveraging existing CSC2 and S&RCS tools under the AFC2ISRC charter. This lead role would need to be supported by the AFC2ISRC/CC and A4/7 (formerly AF/IL) and the AFC2ISRC mission statement might need to be revised to emphasize the importance of the CSC2 and S&RCS development responsibility. Staffing levels to accomplish the new responsibilities may need to be reviewed to ensure that they are adequate to handle the added responsibilities.

The technologies associated with S&RL are still in an early stage of development and may not be fielded for a number of years. Ultimately, the CSC2 system should relate how CS performance and resource levels affect operations, but current theoretical understanding limits these relationships. Of the industry applications surveyed, the General Electric Expert-On-Alert locomotive application comes the closest to providing a true S&R capability; however, it is focused on the physical phenomena associated with engine failures. The prediction of engine failures based on physical observations is a much simpler problem than determining the effect of many interrelated logistics systems on operational effects. The Air Force does not appear to be lagging behind industry in the implementation of S&RL capabilities but should continue to make judicious investments in this field, with a view to testing these applications within the CSC2 framework.

Finally, the observations of the Joint Logistics Transformation Forum are worth repeating: Unless significant improvements are made to "last-mile" transportation in-theater, S&RL will have only a limited effect on operations. A robust, assured transportation network is the foundation on which expeditionary operations, as well as S&RL implementation, rests. The complete integration of transportation into the CSC2 architecture is essential.

Bibliography

ACC Regional Supply Squadron, transcript of interview, Langley Air Force Base, Va., February 6, 2001.

Aerospace Command and Control, Intelligence, Surveillance, and Reconnaissance Center, *AF Command and Control CONOPs,* Vol. III, *Blue Order of Battle, Global Awareness for Expeditionary Aerospace Forces,* Langley Air Force Base, Va., July 7, 2000.

Adams John L., John B. Abell, and Karen Isaacson, *Modeling and Forecasting the Demand for Aircraft Recoverable Spare Parts,* Santa Monica, Calif.: RAND Corporation, R-4211-AF/OSD, 1993.

AFRL/HEAL, Team-Based Assessment of Socio-Technical Logistics (TASL) point paper.

"Agent Technology Roadmap: Overview and Consultation Report," Agentlink III, December 2004. Online at www.agentlink.org.

Alberts, David S., John J. Garstka, Richard E. Hayes, and David A. Signori, *Understanding Information Age Warfare,* Washington, D.C.: Department of Defense Command and Control Research Program Publication Series, 2001.

Amouzegar, Mahyar A., Lionel A. Galway, and Amanda Geller, *Supporting Expeditionary Aerospace Forces: Alternatives for Jet Engine Intermediate Maintenance,* Santa Monica, Calif.: RAND Corporation, MR-1431-AF, 2002.

Amouzegar, Mahyar A., Lionel A. Galway, and Robert S. Tripp, "Integrated Logistics Planning for Expeditionary Aerospace Force," *Journal of Operational Research,* Vol. 55, 2004.

Amouzegar, Mahyar A., Robert S. Tripp, Ronald G. McGarvey, Edward Wei-Min Chan, and Charles Robert Roll, Jr., *Supporting Air and Space Expeditionary Forces: Analysis of Combat Support Basing Options*, Santa Monica, Calif.: RAND Corporation, MG-261-AF, 2004.

Amouzegar, Mahyar A., Ronald G. McGarvey, Robert S. Tripp, Louis Luangkesorn, Thomas Lang, and C. Robert Roll, Jr., *Evaluation of Options for Overseas Combat Support Basing*, Santa Monica, Calif.: RAND Corporation, MG-421-AF, 2006.

Boeing Aircraft Company, "Boeing Demonstrates Ways to Reduce Joint Strike Fighter Maintenance, Life-Cycle Costs," June 28, 2000. Online at www.defense-aerospace.com.

Bonabeau, E., "Agent-Based Modeling: Methods and Techniques for Simulating Human Systems," *Proceedings of the National Academy of Sciences*, Vol. 99 (suppl. 3), 2002.

Bonabeau, E., C. W. Hunt, and P. Gaudiano, "Agent-Based Modeling for Testing and Designing Novel Decentralized Command and Control System Paradigms," presented at the 8th International Command and Control Research and Technology Symposium, Washington, D.C.: National Defense University, June 17–19, 2003.

Bowersox, D. J., D. J. Closs, and C. T. Hall, "Beyond ERP, the Storm Before the Calm," *Supply Chain Management Review*, Vol. 1, 1998.

Brown, Bernice B., *Characteristics of Demand for Aircraft Spare Parts*, Santa Monica, Calif.: RAND Corporation, R-292, 1956.

Camm, Frank A., and Leslie Lewis, *Effective Treatment of Logistics Resource Issues in the Air Force Planning, Programming, and Budgeting (PPBS) System Process*, Santa Monica, Calif.: RAND Corporation, MR-1611-AF, 2003

Carley, K. M., Computational Organization Science: A New Frontier, *Proceedings of the National Academy of Sciences*, Vol. 9, 2002. Online at http://www.pnas.org/cgi/content/abstract/99/suppl_3/7257.

Davidsson, P., L. Henesey, L. Ramstedt, J. Törnquist, and F. Wernstedt, "Agent-Based Approaches to Transport Logistics," *Proceedings of the 3rd International Joint Conference on Autonomous Agents and Multi-Agent Systems, Workshop on Agents in Traffic and Transportation*, New York, 2004.

Defense Advanced Research Projects Agency, "Ultra-Log Brief by DARPA." Online at http://dtsn.darpa.mil/ixo/ (as of June 20, 2005).

Epstein, Joshua M., "Agent-Based Computational Models and Generative Social Science," *Complexity*, Vol. 4, No. 5, 1999.

Feeney, G. J., James W. Peterson, and Craig C. Sherbrooke, *An Aggregate Base Stockage Policy for Recoverable Spare Parts*, Santa Monica, Calif.: RAND Corporation, RM-3644-PR, 1963.

Feinberg, Amatzia, Hyman L. Shulman, Louis W. Miller, and Robert S. Tripp, *Supporting Expeditionary Aerospace Forces: Expanded Analysis of LANTIRN Options*, Santa Monica, Calif.: RAND Corporation, MR-1225-AF, 2001.

Galway, Lionel A., Robert S. Tripp, Timothy L. Ramey, and John G. Drew, *Supporting Expeditionary Aerospace Forces: New Agile Combat Support Postures*, Santa Monica, Calif.: RAND Corporation, MR-1075-AF, 2000

Geisler, M. A., B. B. Brown, and O. M. Hixon, *Analysis of B-47 Consumption Data and Activity*, Santa Monica, Calif.: RAND Corporation, RM-1288, 1954a.

Geisler, Murray A., and John William Theodore Youngs, *Predictability of Demand for B-47 Airframe Spares Items*, Santa Monica, Calif.: RAND Corporation, RM-1300, 1954b.

Geller, Amanda, David George, Robert S. Tripp, Mahyar A. Amouzegar, and Charles Robert Roll, Jr., *Supporting Expeditionary Aerospace Forces: Analysis of Maintenance Forward Support Location Operations*, Santa Monica, Calif.: RAND Corporation, MG-151-AF, 2004.

Haeckel, Stephan H., "Managing by Wire: Using I/T to Transform a Business from 'Make and Sell' to 'Sense-and-Respond,'" in Jerry N. Luftman, ed., *Competing in the Information Age: Strategic Alignment in Practice*, New York: Oxford University Press, Inc., 1996.

———, *Adaptive Enterprise: Creating and Leading Sense-and-Respond Organizations*, Boston, Mass.: Harvard Business School Press, 1999.

Hanser, Lawrence M., Maren Leed, and Charles Robert Roll, The Warfighting Capacity of Air Combat Command's Numbered Air Forces, Santa Monica, Calif.: RAND Corporation, DB-297-AF, 2000.

Headquarters 7AF, 7AF staff, transcript of email interviews, Osan Air Base, Korea, December 10–11, 2001.

Headquarters, 13AF, Andersen Air Force Base, Guam, December 13–14, 2001.

Headquarters, Air Combat Command, ACC Crisis Action Team and LG staff, transcript of interview, Langley Air Force Base, Va., February 6, 2001.

Headquarters Air Force Materiel Command, XPAO, transcript of interview, Wright-Patterson Air Force Base, Ohio, February 21, 2001a.

———, Battle Staff, transcript of interview, May 2, 2001b.

———, "Draft VICP CONOPS," February 6, 2003.

Headquarters, CENTAF, A-4 Supply, transcript of interview, Shaw Air Force Base, S.C., February 7, 2001a.

———, AFFOR A-4, transcript of interview, Shaw Air Force Base, S.C., February 8, 2001b.

———, AFFOR A-3/A-5, transcript of interview, Shaw Air Force Base, S.C., February 8, 2001c.

———, AFFOR A-4, transcript of interview, Shaw Air Force Base, S.C., April 25–26, 2001d.

———, A-7, transcript of interview, Shaw Air Force Base, S.C., February 15, 2002.

Headquarters, Joint Chiefs of Staff, J-4, interview, Washington D.C.: Pentagon, February 23, 2001.

Headquarters, PACAF, 52 AOG and LG staff, transcript of interview, Hickam Air Force Base, Hawaii, March 6–9, 2001, December 17–18, 2001.

Headquarters, USAFE, 32 Air Operations Squadron, transcript of interview, Ramstein Air Base, Germany, April 5, 2001.

Headquarters, USAFE, LG staff, transcript of interview, Ramstein Air Base, Germany, April 4, 2001, January 22–24, 2002.

Hengartner, N., and M. Blume-Kohout "Why Social Networks Matter: Insufficiency of Homogeneous Mixing for Epidemic Models," paper presented at the Conference on Quantitative Methods and Statistical Applications in Defense and National Security, Santa Monica, Calif.: RAND Corporation, February 2006.

Hillestad, R. J., *Dyna-METRIC: Dynamic Multi-Echelon Technique for Recoverable Item Control*, Santa Monica, Calif.: RAND Corporation, R-2785-AF, 1982.

Hollywood, John S., Diane Snyder, Kenneth McKay, and John E. Boon, *Out of the Ordinary: Finding Hidden Threats By Analyzing Unusual Behavior*, Santa Monica, Calif.: RAND Corporation, MG-126-RC, 2004.

Illachinski, Andrew, *Artificial War: Multiagent-Based Simulation of Combat*, Singapore: World Scientific Publishing, 2004.

Joint Chiefs of Staff, *DoD Dictionary of Military and Associated Terms*, Joint Pub 1-02, Washington D.C., April 12, 2001.

———, *Focused Logistics Campaign Plan*, 2004. Online at https://acc.dau/mil/simplify/ev.php?ID=52053_201&ID2=DO_TOPIC.

Joint Logistics Transformation Forum, Office of the Deputy Under Secretary of Defense (Logistics and Materiel Readiness), Washington, D.C., April 25–26, 2005.

Leftwich, James, Robert S. Tripp, Amanda Geller, Patrick H. Mills, Tom LaTourrette, Charles Robert Roll, Jr., Cauley Von Hoffman, and David Johansen, *Supporting Expeditionary Aerospace Forces: An Operational Architecture for Combat Support Execution Planning and Control*, Santa Monica, Calif.: RAND Corporation, MR-1536-AF, 2002.

Lempert, R. A., "New Decision Sciences for Complex Systems," *Proceedings of the National Academy of Sciences*, Vol. 99 (suppl. 3), 2002.

Lin, Grace, Steve Buckley, Heng Cao, Nathan Caswell, Markus Ettl, Shubir Kapoor, Lisa Koenig, Kaan Katircioglu, Anil Nigam, Bala Ramachandran, and Ko-Yang Wang, "The Sense-and-Respond Enterprise: IBM Researchers Develop Integrated SAR System of Global Value Chain Optimization," *OR/MS Today*, April 2002.

Luck, Michael, Peter McBurney, Onn Shehory, and Steve Willmott, *Agency Technology Roadmap: A Roadmap for Agent Based Computing*, Southampton, UK: University of Southampton (on behalf of AgentLink III), 2005.

Lynch, Kristin F., John G. Drew, Robert S. Tripp, and C. Robert Roll, Jr., *Supporting Air and Space Expeditionary Forces: Lessons from Operation Iraqi Freedom*, Santa Monica, Calif.: RAND Corporation, MG-193-AF, 2005.

McArthur, D., P. Klahr, S. Narain, *ROSS: An Object-Oriented Language for Constructing Simulations*, Santa Monica, Calif.: RAND Corporation, R-3160-AF, 1984.

Menotti, Mark, "The Sense-and-Respond Enterprise: Why the U.S. Marine Corps Should Embrace the New Paradigm," *OR/MS Today*, August 2004.

Meyer, Mark, "The Features and Facets of the Agent Building and Learning Environment (ABLE)," Software Developer, TravelClick, Inc., October 6, 2004. Online at http://www.128.ibm.com/developerworks/autonomic/library/ac-able1/.

Miller, Bruce L., *A Real Time METRIC for the Distribution of Serviceable Assets*, Santa Monica, Calif.: RAND Corporation, RM-5687-PR 1968.

Miller, Charles E., *Airlift Doctrine*, Maxwell AFB, Ala.: Air University Press, March 1988.

Mills, Patrick, Ken Evers, Donna Kinlin, and Robert S. Tripp, *Supporting Air and Space Expeditionary Forces: Expanded Operational Architecture for Combat Support Execution Planning and Control*, Santa Monica, Calif.: RAND Corporation, MG-316-AF, 2006.

Muckstadt, J. A., *Consolidated Support Model (CSM): A Three-Echelon, Multi-Item Model for Recoverable Items*, Santa Monica, Calif.: RAND Corporation, R-1923-PR, 1976.

Newkirk Bryan T., and Karen Currie, *Global Combat Support System: A Must for the Joint Warfighting Commander*, Air Force Journal of Logistics, Vol. XXVII, No. 3, 2005.

PACAF Regional Supply Squadron, transcript of interview, Hickam Air Force Base, Hawaii, March 8, 2001.

Parunak, H.V.D., *Agents in Overalls: Experiences and Issues in the Development and Deployment of Industrial Agent-Based Systems*, Ann Arbor, Mich.: ERIM Center for Electronic Commerce, 1999.

Peltz, Eric, Hyman L. Shulman, Robert S. Tripp, Timothy L. Ramey, Randy King, and John G. Drew, *Supporting Expeditionary Aerospace Forces: An Analysis of F-15 Avionics Options*, Santa Monica, Calif.: RAND Corporation, MR-1174-AF, 2000.

Perugini, Don, Dale Lambert, Leon Sterling, and Adrian Pearce, "Agents for Military Logistic Planning," paper presented at a workshop "Agent Technology in Logistics," *15th European Conference on Artificial Intelligence (ECAI-2202)*, Lyon, France, 2002.

Pyles, Raymond, *The Dyna-METRIC Readiness Assessment Model: Motivation, Capabilities, and Use*, Santa Monica, Calif.: RAND Corporation, R-2886-AF, 1984.

Pyles, Raymond, and Robert S. Tripp, *Measuring and Managing Readiness: The Concept and Design of the Combat Support Capability Management System*, Santa Monica, Calif.: RAND Corporation, N-1840-AF, 1982.

Rainey, James C., Mahyar A. Amouzegar, Beth F. Scott, Robert S. Tripp, Ann M. C. Gayer, eds., *Combat Support: Shaping Air Force Logistics for the 21st Century*, Alabama: Air Force Logistics Management Agency Publisher, August 2003.

Roberti, Mark, "RFID Aided Marines in Iraq," *RFID Journal*, February 21, 2005.

Ryan, General Michael E., U.S. Air Force, "Aerospace Expeditionary Force: Better Use of Aerospace Power for the 21st Century," briefing, Washington, D.C.: U.S. Air Force, 1998.

Schelling, T. C., *Micromotives and Macrobehavior*, New York: Norton, 1978.

Science Applications International Corporation, *The Sense and Respond Logistics Capability and Operation Iraqi Freedom*, n.d.

Sheffi, Yosef, *The Resilient Enterprise: Overcoming Vulnerability for Competitive Advantage*, Cambridge, Mass.: MIT Press, 2005.

Snyder, Don, and Patric H. Mills, *Supporting Air and Space Expeditionary Forces: A Methodology for Determining Air Force Deployment Requirements*, Santa Monica, Calif.: RAND Corporation, MG-176-AF, 2004.

Snyder, Don, Patrick H. Mills, Manuel J. Carrillo, and Adam Resnick, *Supporting Air and Space Expeditionary Forces: Capabilities and Sustainability of Air and Space Expeditionary Forces*, Santa Monica, Calif.: RAND Corporation, MG-303-AF, 2006.

Sullivan, Kevin, Major General, "Concept *to* Reality,*" in James C. Rainey et al., eds., *Combat Support: Shaping Air Force Logistics for the 21st Century*, Ala.: Air Force Logistics Management Agency, August 2003.

Trebilcock, Bob, "Modern Materials Handling," October 2004. Online at www.mmh.com.

Tripp, Robert S., and Larry B. Rainey, "Cybernetics: A Theoretical Foundation for Developing Logistics Information and Control Systems," *The Logistics Spectrum*, Vol. 190, No. 2, Summer 1985.

Tripp, Robert S., Lionel A. Galway, Paul S. Killingsworth, Eric Peltz, Timothy L. Ramey, and John G. Drew, *Supporting Expeditionary Aerospace Forces: An Integrated Strategic Agile Combat Support Planning Framework*, Santa Monica, Calif.: RAND Corporation, MR-1056-AF, 1999.

Tripp, Robert S., Lionel A. Galway, Timothy L. Ramey, Mahyar A. Amouzegar, and Eric Peltz, *Supporting Expeditionary Aerospace Forces: A Concept for Evolving to the Agile Combat Support/Mobility System of the Future*, Santa Monica, Calif.: RAND Corporation, MR-1179-AF, 2000.

Tripp, Robert S., Kristin F. Lynch, John G. Drew, and Edward Wei-Min Chan, *Supporting Expeditionary Aerospace Forces: Lessons from Operation Enduring Freedom,* MR-1819-AF, Santa Monica, Calif.: RAND, 2004

U.S. Air Force, *Readiness*, Air Force Policy Directive 10-2, Washington D.C., March 1, 1997a.

———, *Air Force Basic Doctrine*, Air Force Doctrine Document 1, Washington, D.C., September 1, 1997b.

———, *Operation Plan and Concept Plan Development and Implementation*, Air Force Manual 10-401, Washington D.C., May 1, 1998.

———, *Operational Procedures—Aerospace Operations Center*, Air Force Instruction 13-1AOC, Vol. III, Washington D.C., June 1, 1999.

———, *Status of Resources and Training System*, Air Force Instruction 10-201, Washington D.C., May 4, 2000a.

———, *Air Force Vision 2020: Global Vigilance, Reach, and Power,* June 9, 2000b.

———, *Combat Support,* Air Force Doctrine Document 2-4, Washington D.C., October 2000c.

———, "Command and Control," Air Force Doctrine Document 2-8 (draft), Washington D.C., February 16, 2001a.

———, *Organization and Employment of Aerospace Power*, Air Force Doctrine Document 2, Washington D.C., February 17, 2001b.

———, "Expeditionary Logistics for the 21st Century (eLog21) Campaign Plan," 2002.

———, "Joint Expeditionary Forces Experiment 99 Final Report," Air Force Experimentation Office, undated (a). Online at https://jefxlink. langley.AF.mil/.

———, "Joint Expeditionary Forces Experiment 00 Final Report," Air Force Experimentation Office, undated (b). Online at https://jefxlink. langley.AF.mil.

U.S. Department of Defense, *C4ISR Framework Document Version 2.0*, Washington D.C., December 18, 1997.

———, *Joint Vision 2020*, Washington, D.C., June 19, 2000.

———, *Defense Strategy Review*, Washington, D.C., June 21, 2001a.

———, *Guidance and Terms of Reference for the 2001 Quadrennial Defense Review*, Washington, D.C., June 22, 2001b.

———, *Operational Sense and Respond Logistics Concept Development, Analysis, and Proof-of-Concept Capability Integration*, Washington, D.C., 2003.

———, *Sense and Respond Logistics: Co-evolution of and Adaptive Enterprise Capability*, Concept Document (Long Version), Washington, D.C., 2004a.

———, *Operational Sense and Respond Logistics Concept Development, Analysis, and Proof-of-Concept Capability Integration*, Washington, D.C., 2004b.

USA Log Transformation Agency, Sense and Respond Logistics Demonstration Briefing, McClean, Va., March 31, 2005.

USAFE Regional Supply Squadron, transcript of interview, Ramstein Air Force Base, Germany, April 4, 2001.

Willis, Henry H., and David Santana Ortiz, *Evaluating the Security of the Global Containerized Supply Chain*, Santa Monica, Calif.: RAND Corporation, TR-214-RC, 2004.

Wolf, Eric S., *Using Agents to Model Logistics*, 71st MORS Symposium, Composite Group G, MCB Quantico, Va.: Marine Corps University, 2003a.

———, *Using Agent-Based Distillations to Explore Logistics Support to Urban, Humanitarian Assistance/Disaster Relief Operations*, master's degree thesis, Monterey, Calif.: Naval Postgraduate School, 2003b.

Zettler, Michael, Lt. General, *The New Global Vision,* in James C. Rainey et al., eds., *Combat Support: Shaping Air Force Logistics for the 21st Century,* Ala.: Air Force Logistics Management Agency, August 2003.

AMERICAN JESUS

POEMS
BY
RICHARD VARGAS

TIA CHUCHA PRESS
LOS ANGELES

I would like to thank the editors of these publications for previously publishing the following, sometimes in a different version:

Used with permission of copyright holder *Bilingual Review / Editorial Bilingue:*
   "Driving to O'Hare," "For Aunt Connie... With Love" first published in *Bilingual Review,* Vol. 24, No. 3, Arizona State University, Tempe, AZ.

Breakast All Day (BAD) *"9 Men, 25 Women, 14 Children, One Infant," "Whimper"*
Chiron Review *"Racism 101"*
Main Street Rag *"Truer Words," "Soulmate," "Another Nature Poem," "Five Hundred," "Army Poem III & IV"*
Princeton Arts Review *"On The Outside"*
Rattle *"And Yet, Another Nature Poem"*
Rockhurst Review *"How I Became He-Weeps-Fire"*
The Rockford Review *"American Jesus," "It's a Living II"*
Vampire's Ball *"It Happens to the Best of Us"*
Willow Review *"Driving to Platteville"*
Wormwood Review *"I Got Them Dirty Underwear Blues," "The Job, a Swing Shift Lament," "What Does it Mean?"*
Xispas.com *"Spider-Man in Albuquerque"*

ISBN 978-882688-34-0
Book Design: Jane Brunette
Front and Back Cover Photo: Mark Bond

PUBLISHED BY:
Tia Chucha Press
A Project of Tia Chucha's Centro Cultural
PO Box 328
San Fernando, CA 91341
www.tiachucha.com

DISTRIBUTED BY:
Northwestern University Press
Chicago Distribution Center
11030 South Langley Avenue
Chicago, IL 60628

Tia Chucha Press is supported by the National Endowment for the Arts and operating funds from Tia Chucha's Centro Cultural. Tia Chucha's Café & Centro Cultural have received support from Los Angeles County Arts Commission, the Los Angeles Department of Cultural Affairs, Los Angeles Community Redevelopment Agency, Trill Hill Foundation, Panta Rhea Foundation, the Center for Cultural Innovation, the Middleton Foundation, Not Just Us Foundation, the Liberty Hill Foundation, Youth Can Service, Toyota Sales, Solidago Foundation, and other grants and donors including Bruce Springsteen, John Densmore, Dan Attias, Dave Marsh, David Sandoval, Denise Chávez and John Randall of the Border Book Festival, Luis & Trini Rodríguez, and others.

for
Ed Field
poet/mentor/friend

TABLE OF CONTENTS

*"But why should we hear about body bags, and deaths,
and how many, what day it's gonna happen, and how many
this or what do you suppose? Or, I mean, it's, it's not relevant.
So why should I waste my beautiful mind on
something like that?"*

BARBARA BUSH
ON "GOOD MORNING AMERICA,"
MARCH 18, 2003

he walked away from the city
and the bright lights
found a town where a tall
building is considered
anything over two stories
he doesn't miss the super
hero gig
all the bad guys now wear
suits and class rings from
ivy league schools
where's the fun in that?

the closest he came to
helping someone in distress
in his new city was the time
two cops chased a homeless
man away from patio seating at
one of the trendy restaurants
in Nob Hill

he caught up with the guy
gave him a couple of bucks
felt good about it
better than any ass whipping
he ever had to dish out to the
freak of the week

he misses his girl and
the dimple in her wicked
smile when he used to tie
her up with his webbing
practicing various japanese
S&M knots

Maryjane married rich
lives in northern Calif
raises championship horses
hosts republican fundraisers
where the highlight of the
evening is when the band
plays "Tie a Yellow Ribbon..."
and the wealthy get up
to shake their booty

on hot summer nights
he latches on to the top
of a city bus
rides up and down
Central Ave from
the Sandia Mts all
the way downtown

counts a star in the desert
sky for every regret he
ever had and then counts
another one for everytime
he felt like the luckiest
man alive

SOULMATE

the second time we met
at Sonny's bar she was
telling me about the short
stories of Paul Bowles
and how some of them
made her feel high

she said she was going
home to get the book
for me and i'm thinking
"yeah, right..."
but 15 minutes later
she walks back in
puts the book in front
of me on the bar
orders another beer

later
the drunk jailbird
from Arizona who
had been bumming
drinks all night
leans over and asks
if she'd like to go
make out in the
parking lot

the great ones never
miss an opening and i
knew she was something
special when
shaking her head no
she looks at me and
says "i'd rather have
my nipples shaved off
with a cheese grater..."

POOL

many a quarter is lost
until one day at the table
everything comes together
a world defined on dingy
green felt in a smoke hazed
room and everyone is watching
as you seize it
dissect it with some sort of primeval
geometry imbedded in your genes
you sense the elation of those around you
at the sight of a man grasping
control of his destiny for the 1st time
since who-knows-when
the 8 ball gracefully sinking out
of sight ending the game too soon
like a quick and unexpected sunset on one of
those rare days when everything goes right

another quarter goes down
everyone agreeing it's such a small price to pay

SUCCESS... FOR LYNYRD SKYNYRD

sitting in a bar after work
sipping a beer and contemplating the
strange turn my life has taken

everything is going my way
editors no longer send me
one word rejection slips
got promoted at my job
got a date next week
with a woman who has been
the leading lady in my dreams for
the last three months

when out of nowhere the jukebox
comes on with a song by one of my
favorite bands
their last plane ride together
left them scattered all over
the countryside like so many
pieces of the Colonel's chicken
tossed out the window
of a speeding r.v.

finishing my beer
i get up to leave and
outside the evening rain
has transformed the street's
blacktop surface into a slick
stretch of relocated runway

and while still remembering you
i fasten my seatbelt

hope for the best

KNOW THE FEELING?

don't say you never
know what it's like
to have so much
love inside and
nowhere to put it

so much trying
to get out it
makes you cry
while staring into
the monitor on your desk
riding the bus downtown
or eating eggs and bacon
in your favorite diner
surrounded by people
all feeling just like you do
but no one willing to make
the first move

until one day
while watching tv
or taking a nap on the couch
you double over
as it punches its way out
rips open your beer belly
like a baby alien
but now it's changed
mutated into something else
innocent and vicious
starved for affection
it begins to feed and grow

your last thought
before succumbing to
the shock and the pain
is of the crazy world
we live in and how
it finally

all makes sense

the greatest compliment
i ever got was from Cecil Wall
a combat vet from Korea and
two tours in Nam
he was black as
midnight without the moon
bald head slick
like a pair of his spit
shined boots
his beer keg chest
decorated with battle scars
permanent reminders of
beating the odds when it
counted the most

you couldn't miss the nasty
one on his neck and he would
only tell you once about being
paralyzed on his back
the only sounds he could hear
were charlie's footsteps moving
through the elephant grass and
the gurgling of blood
spurting from his throat
when out of nowhere a
buddy picked him up
slung him over and double-
timed their asses outta
harm's way just like in
the movies but then again
where do you think they
get this stuff?

and he would tell you about
coming home
how good it felt to be back
even if the welcome of a grateful
nation was out of the question
then the riots in Detroit
erupted and his unit was
deployed to patrol the streets
where he was shot at by his
own people and i'll never forget
how he stared off into space
said in a tone cold as death
"fuck it... it was like being back
in Nam, and we acted accordingly..."
then he would pick up his
CC&7 and down it with
one gulp

it was during one such episode
as we were drinking back at
my place
a farewell of sorts as my reporting
date for OCS drew near
First Sergeant Wall finished
his drink then held out his
empty glass
i mixed him another as he started
talking about leaders and assholes
and the fine line that separates
the two

then he said it
words i will carry with me
until i breathe my last
"Corporal Vahhhgus, i'd
follow you into battle.
i know i'd be alright with you..."

ask yourself how many times
in a life does a man turn to
you proclaiming his blind
trust in your judgement when
the worst kind of shit
hits the biggest fan
pulls his bloody heart from
his chest and puts it in your
hands for safekeeping

for most of us
it will never happen
but if it does
handle the moment
with respect and care

to be considered
a gift
a delicate
silence
to be broken
only

by the sound
of clinking ice

IT HAPPENS TO THE BEST OF US

she's turning pale
whiter than a sheet in a Chlorox commercial
refuses to come out during the day
has stopped wearing underwear
under long clingy gowns
revealing curves and crevices
you still long to kiss
sensing she desperately wants
to pull you close you reach
for her only to notice her
inner struggle to keep you
at arm's length
"no... no! i can't! i still love you..."
as she opens the door to her apt
sends you home to another
cold shower or mary palm
and her five sisters

lately
you've caught her staring
at your neck
dark eyes transfixed
with hunger and lust
saliva drips from the corner
of her mouth as the tip of
a tongue red as passion
fruit barely parts her lips

on the day you're wondering
why she's taken down
all her mirrors including the
one on the medicine cabinet
she calls you on the phone to say
she can't see you anymore
weeps as she says it's over

"but babe, we can work it out..."
"no! you must stay away
for your own good... promise!"
she hangs up and when you
drop by after work her place
is empty with no forwarding
address to be found

and just like that
she's walked out of your
life forever leaving you to
pick up the pieces
you want to join the marines
leave the country
swipe razor blades
across both wrists
but time does heal all
wounds until she only
haunts your sleep and
the memories about
the good times you both
shared begin to fade
like old dreams

a year later you're standing in line
with your new girl waiting to get in
for the Rolling Stones farewell concert
as you check out the stretch limos
pulling up and the VIPs using the
special entrance she steps out of one
glowing translucent like a statue
chiseled from polar ice
she's wearing a designer gown
fitting like a second skin
that would set you back
two months pay
her escort is just as cold
looks like a model you saw

in Esquire magazine
except this guy
drips testosterone
and even though he's
wearing shades his chilling
smile reminds you of a
great white rising to the
surface where you float
on your board waiting
for the next wave
then you realize
he's staring right
at you

and somehow
deep inside
you know
things have
turned out
for the best

Five Hundred

the news made it sound
like something to get
excited about

we tend to think of
the number as a milestone
Barry Bonds hitting home runs
a sitcom still on the air
a fast food conglomerate
opening one more drive-thru

but i imagine planes
landing and expelling
dark military issue coffins
from their deep hollow
bellies
a detail of soldiers
greeting them one by one
the white gloves they wear
on their hands making it
easy to follow as they
surrender the crisp motion
required for a proper
salute

they may not let us
see them arriving
cold and alone
but there is a stench
in the air
and no matter
how many times
we bathe

it won't wash off

it's the day after Jesus' birthday
the devout have come to see
how much they can save on marked
down Christmas cards and wrapping paper
these post-holiday locusts looking
for the crumbs they missed

the picture in today's
paper shows the coffins lined up
mourners in the Chiapas sun
beating their breasts
9 men, 25 women, 14 children, one infant
greeted with bullets and machetes on their
way to worship a complacent god

"how much are these cards with the discount?"
but i don't answer
ignore this american cow
with too much makeup and a cheap dye job
instead i hear the sound of a mountain
breeze rustling trees
or is it the wheeze of a sucking
chest wound

"i need to exchange this, do i have
to get in that long line?"
no you don't
you can come with me and walk along
this stream of fresh water
cool and crisp
ponder its bubbling song
washing over ancient rocks
or is that wet noise
a child choking on its own blood

"how long is this sale going to last?"
as long as human lives
can be bought and sold
traded and smuggled
stomped on and swept under the rug
in a world where precious metals
and shiny rocks outweigh your worth
or mine

finally i answer feeling the tears
forming in the corners of my eyes
"these cards were originally priced at $10.50,
and with the sale price you save $5.25."
the customer is happy
corporate is happy
America is happy
everyone is happy except

9 men, 25 women, 14 children,
and one infant

RECONQUEST

his ghost walks the vacant aisles late at night
eating a bag of doritos and drinking
a coke he pauses in sporting goods
admires the hunting knives under the
glass case and remembers how it felt
to hold a man's warm beating
heart in his hand

now
his sons have swapped
jaguar skins and quetzal feathers
for retail blue
their new war cry
stenciled on their backs

his daughters are sacrificed
their corpses found randomly
in the desert
tortured burned and mutilated
tributes to the new gods of
free trade and open markets

he stands amid the cheap
merchandise as outside
blue plastic bags
cling to nearby
fences waving
in the wind like
a new national flag

unlike the benevolent feathered serpent
it has replaced
this one is coiled tight
as it takes its place in the shadow

of the great pyramid
ready to strike without warning

here to stay
for a long
long time

WATCHING MY OLD MAN KICK SOMEONE'S ASS

i was three maybe four
looked out the screen door
there he was across the street
people were standing in a circle
he and another man were in the middle
my old man must have been in his early 20s
lean hard and mean
fresh out of the 82nd airborne
the other guy was soft
a pendejo who never left the block
my dad was throwing his shit
left and right
his opponent was backing up into
the crowd losing his footing
but afraid to take his eyes off
the crazy cholo coming at him
it was over before it really started
my old man victorious and cocky
i remember he looked from
across the street
saw me standing in the doorway
our eyes met and i knew he had
just shown me something important
i took a mental snapshot
so i'd always carry
the moment with me

now
when i want to strike out
unleash the blow we all
have within us
i write a poem

and i know
he would
approve

END-OF-TIMES SEX

first
we'll be freaked
struggle with the necessities
food water shelter
the cost of a scarce roll
of our favorite toilet paper
will make the coin we pay
for a gallon of gas look like
pocket change
but after the great adaptation
after we find our groove
as our species always does
our attention will turn to
the more important things

by the light of a precious
candle we'll remember the
art of undressing each other
the tease of a zipper pulled
oh so slow
the thrill of balancing her calf
in one hand while sucking her
little toe gently like
a ripe and delicate grape
our tongues will go places
they almost forgot
purring like cats will
become a natural response
as naked skin glides
across naked skin

then
taking a break between the warm sheets
tearing open a package of oreos
from our emergency disaster stash
feeding them to each other

discovering the joy of taking turns
licking the crumbs off our partner's backside
we'll wonder aloud what the hell we were
supposed to be afraid of
and why?

we were taking a break between clutches
in the Motel 6 darkness,
waiting for our second wind.
when, for no reason at all, she started.
1st, i heard about the episode with a perfect stranger
in San Diego, a hitchhiker who turned her on
to some acid, and left her in the backseat of her car
at a local drive-in, her panties on backwards.
then, there was the middle-aged, recently divorced
business executive who kept falling asleep
despite the romantic fireplace setting and
a hundred and twenty dollar a night view
of the beach.
this led to her 1st time, a high school jock
who came in three seconds and asked her if she
was alright.
the clincher, though, was the one night stand who led
her to believe that he was single, and while wrestling
between the sheets at his place, what should her feet
get tangled in except for a pair of his wife's dirty
underwear.

i sat up, wondered what she would say about me,
the poet with a pecker shrinking like an
elongated balloon with a slow leak.

HOW I KNOW THERE IS A GOD

some people go to church on Sunday
but i always preferred the
Coliseum in downtown L.A.
my old man took me there to see
my first pro game when i was 5 yrs old
saw Fran Tarkenton and his new team
in purple beat our beloved Rams
i learned new four lettered words that day
it was imbedded into my young
developing male consciousness
that ol' Fran was a prick
an opinion i've never been
able to shake

through the decades i went there often
becoming one with the concession stands
the sweet aroma of foot long hot dogs
and cold beer topped with foam
the scalpers brazenly holding tickets
in the air to get my attention
the hundred charcoal fires burning
in the parking lot as gray smoke drifted
overhead and the smells of bar-b-que
and carne asada hung heavy in the
hot September air like a working man's
incense

the Coliseum is sacred ground, man
sacred

the last NFL team to call it home
were the Raiders
a team that used to be able to win
when the odds were stacked against them
but since their last Super Bowl

victory in '83 have hit hard times
stayed in pause mode while the
rest of the league hit fast forward
but i love them anyway
always went to a game feeling
they would finally awaken and prevail

on this particular gameday
they were up to their usual
as they fumbled
got penalized
and gave the other team enough
breaks to win the game just
for showing up

making matters worse
i had a couple of obnoxious drunks
sitting in front of me wearing
Chicago Bears' jerseys who were
providing biting commentary
taunting the hometown fans on their
own turf and breaking up into hysterics
when the Raider QB threw a pass
end over end that fell like a block
of concrete 10 yds. short of the
intended target
then they said they came on a bus
outta Vegas and had a shit-wad of
dough bet against my team and afterwards
they would be chugging cold ones all the
way back to collect their winnings

during the last 10 minutes of the game
while i contemplated making a dash
for the car and beating the traffic
this old guy gets up at the end of the
row of seats in front of me and stumbles
doing a great Dean Martin imitation

the two Bears fans had to stand
so the guy could pass
as he ascended the steps to
the exit tunnel weaving back and forth
my tormentors took a double take
and one said to the other
"holy shit, did you see who that was?
that was our bus driver... we're fucked!"

as they ran up the stairs to check on
the guy who was supposed to get
them home safe and sound
i took a long swallow from my
warm beer and decided to watch
the end of the game

smiled to myself
as i realized this was better
than a burning bush

and 10 times more convincing

THIS REALLY HAPPENED

i was at this drive-in movie watching
this flick and holding back from going to
the john for at least a 1/2 hour because i
didn't want to miss any good parts.

(like the scene where this broad's eyes
get poked out by a big black bird, and she
stumbles onto the highway and gets pulverized
by this whining diesel...actually showed it
in slow motion.)

finally, when there seemed to be a lull
in the action, i decided to make a break for it.
as i grabbed the door handle, a voice interrupted
the movie and said,
"peter schmuck, please come to the snack bar,
peter schmuck, please come to the snack bar."

i heard the couple parked next to me giggle,
and someone said, "who the fuck is peter schmuck?"

well, what would you have done?
i waited another fifteen minutes.

ARMY POEM II

Joe the XO graduated from
West Point but you'd never
know it because he was
top heavy for an infantry
officer with a W.C. Fields
nose and surfer blonde hair
looked like a young Santa
minus the beard

when training in the field
after the mess tent was
situated and the fueling
schedule for the company's
vehicles was set he always
found the nearest fishing hole
finding the time to cast
a line or two while filling
an empty c-ration can with
dark brown tobacco juice

his favorite story was how
one night in the dark he meant
to reach for the k-y jelly but
grabbed the vicks vapo-rub instead
his depiction of how he and
the little lady started to scream
once they got going always left
us with tears in our eyes

so you can imagine my surprise
the day he pulled me aside
pointed to one of our sergeants
and said "ever notice how some
of these guys look like monkeys?"
the oblivious smile on his face

reminding me how sad i felt
the day i realized George Allen
really was blackballed from
coaching in the NFL
or when they killed off the Duke
at the end of *The Cowboys*

at the end of the day
i went back to my room
soaked in a tub of water
as hot as i could stand it
sipped a cold beer
lit a cigar

scrubbed my skin
raw
knew i wouldn't
feel clean for
a long time

FOR OLIVIA, DYING

funny
always thought i'd be there
at your side
the dutiful son holding your hand
but now it's relief i feel
half way across the country and
finally able to stand straight
as the weight slips from my shoulders

i remember well the life lessons you gave me
how to discard family relations like used candy wrappers
the ability to turn the heart into a piece of coal
how to be desperate for the good life
and give your children a deaf ear
as they cry out in the dark shadow
of a stepfather's lewd smile

i know the fear that motivates an animal
to gnaw its own leg off
run and stumble into the night
get far away as possible

now, after many years of trying to unlearn
what i can never forget
i return the favor
present a life lesson of my own
from me to you

when the pain is so unbearable
my name cursed for not showing
the respect you thought was your maternal right
remember this:

certain flowers survive the freezing kiss of December
thrive in the smothering heat of August

they can be pulled out
mowed under
spitted and shitted on

yet
when least expected
they will still rise up to the sun
and bloom

when lunch time comes around,
we head out to the parking lot,
a migratory herd of caribous looking for greener pastures.
we pull out our pipes, our papers, our smoke.
we talk about getting fucked by the bossman,
the union,
our women.
and always the new job we're going to go out looking
for tomorrow.

when we return to the warehouse,
the old guys sitting down with cups of
coffee in their hands notice our arrival,
smelling the lingering smoke and saying nothing.
these oldtimers with the thick skin of a rhino's hide
have known the pain.
they look the other way.
and in our silence
we know it's just a matter of time.

the girl on stage had the face of a young
Mayan princess, the body of a playboy centerfold.
tugging at her black bikini bottoms,
she smiled at me.
and if i'd had it to bargain with, my soul would
have been hers.

which brings to mind my 8th grade english teacher
and the time she kept me after class to discuss
something i had written. she paced back and forth
in front of my desk, looking like a conviction
crazed prosecutor warming up for the kill.
she waved my composition in front of my face
like it was a piece of prized evidence.
"this bit about looking up the girl's dress
in your math class... what does it mean?"

she caught me by surprise, and i just sat there
like a startled jackrabbit, blinded by a pair of
approaching headlights.

SCARIEST DREAM EVER

woke up
stumbled to
the bathroom
to pee
turned on light
pulled down shorts
screamed

Nike Swoosh
on the head
of my dick

Reincarnating

people in India call me
they are paid to call me
they have names like Justin
or Megan and when i ask
they can't tell me
where they are
calling from
it's not authorized
information

but they have soft
exotic accents and
a polite tone of voice
i derive satisfaction
knowing they will
make lousy bill
collectors
they ask why i'm
not paying my Visa bill
i tell them i can't find
a decent job
they are silent
like someone trying
to tiptoe around a
minefield

they want to make it
easy for me and pre-
arrange payment
all they need is my
checking account
number and
this is how it starts

then they will want
all my sexual fantasies
and my I.Q.
my shoe size
and my favorite color
what food gives me heartburn
did i ever air guitar to a song
by Led Zepplin and if so
which one
when did i lose my virginity
and who did i vote for
in the last election
slowly i'll begin
to vanish
disappear
like the invisible man
until one day
i'll lay down at night
only to wake up
on the banks of
a mighty river
dark people with
beautiful white teeth
will pull me to the
muddy brown waters
urge me to bathe
and pray

i will say the strange names
of gods i don't know
launch delicate bouquets
of red and gold flowers
that drift slowly out of sight
feel like i had something
important to do
but can't remember
what it was

THE PASSION 2004

stripped
beaten
pulled by the rope
around his neck
he ends up posed
with his arms stretched
wide and his head hanging
low as he awaits his fate while
all around him fair skinned
soldiers from an occupying army
sent by the western world
to save him from himself
and secure his country's
natural resources
make jokes about his
dark brown penis
someone drapes Mary
Magdalene's panties
over his head to be
worn like a thorny
crown

our sons and
daughters are bored
take photos for posterity
and the internet
wearily suck on
cigarettes while
wondering when they
can go home

the only thing missing
is the rolling of dice

You Don't Speak For Me, Cindy

don't speak for me
when you refuse to
accept the reasons
your son had to die

don't speak for me
when you demand
our holy roller leader
with his blacked out
military records
look you in the eye
and say once again
how he understands
your pain

don't speak for me
when the mobs try
to string you up with
red white & blue
rope and treating
you fair and balanced
means putting a
target on your back
and front

don't speak for me, Cindy
i want you to

scream

SICK CALL

the time between
them is getting shorter
the days when i can't do
it anymore
stare at a monitor for 8-10 hrs
taking calls while counting
the minutes between breaks
until the shift ends
and i walk out the door
feeling numb and frustrated
like i've been masturbating
continuously without release
remembering the countless days
of mowing
cooking
selling
loading
warehousing
supervising
delivering
servicing
cashiering
learning the arts of bullshit
and kissing ass for
a cave
a chunk of meat
a fire to keep me warm
and dry

but this is also an art onto itself
as i practice my best
George Burns imitation
my throat turning into a piece
of gravelled road
my breathing becomes labored

like a man pulling himself out of
his deathbed as i call the boss
interlace my voice with suppressed
suffering and a hint of regret
once the deed is done
i make some coffee
turn on the tv
maybe write a poem
that's been banging around
in my head
take a shower
go out for some breakfast
sometimes ride a bus downtown
catch an early matinee

it's like finding something
valuable that you thought
you'd lost

or even better
stealing it back

sometimes our fate is already set
we go along for the ride waiting
for the accident to happen

seeing her for the first time
tied up and helpless
her screams reaching high notes
i didn't think were possible
the full moon's light bouncing
off her shiny yellow hair
those perky breasts ready
to pop out of her Banana
Republic white cotton shirt
well... who could resist?
i knew she was a keeper
even when she fainted and peed
on herself upon seeing lil' Kong
standing firm and erect
begging for her soft touch

always the eternal optimist
i refused to let her go
having her in my hand beat
humping my favorite rock
back at the cave anyday
but you see where this
is going

how many times do we
walk the path of
painful uncertainty
condemn the heart to be
thrown into the air

a grenade with
the pin pulled

hoping it will be
different
this time

so the day i found myself higher
than i'd ever been
looking out over a concrete
and steel horizon
strange lines and shapes making me
realize i'd arrived at a place
where i could never belong
i asked myself
"what do i do now?"
as if on cue
i heard the distant beating
of the drums
having led me here
now calling me back

i took a long gaze upon the
city i was leaving
looked down upon the woman
never meant to return my love
dreams die hard
sometimes we die with them
but when the drums call
wherever you are
whatever you're doing
hold your head high
swallow back the regret
rising in your throat

let go
and don't
look back

KILLING MEXICANS... FOR ESEQUIEL HERNANDEZ

in this country marines
kill mexicans tending sheep
because they look like
drug dealers, terrorists
or worse, illegal landscapers

in this country laws are being passed
to wipe our culture from the land
in California they call them propositions
one of the definitions of the word is
"a request for sexual intercourse"
so i guess this means they are being polite
asking for our permission
before they screw us

in this country
they want us to speak
only english
the official language
of the done deal
the broken treaty
the limp handshake
a tv politician's promise

in this country
we are taking back
the land one minimum
wage job at a time
laughing at their
Taco Bell paranoias
and sour cream fears

they are building walls
to keep us out
but the joke's on them

we never
left

AMERICAN JESUS

leads us into the new crusades
kicks open Muslim doors
under cover of darkness
gives the frightened children
chocolate bars with wrappers
depicting the father, the son
and the half dead vice-president

he multiplies a loaf of Wonder Bread
and a couple of cans of tuna into
M-16s, tanks, and planes
drops a bomb for every man
woman and child refusing our
holy gifts of crooked democracy
and tainted freedom

his disciples spend money
that hasn't been printed yet
they urge us to be patriotic
start Christmas shopping
in June

American Jesus invites us
to the real Last Supper
and this time
the flesh
we eat
the blood
we drink
will be our
own

Army Poem III

the guy hated the army
but his rich old man said he couldn't
claim his share of the family fortune
unless he made something of himself
he'd been kicked out of four schools
catering to the brats of the uppercrust
so this was his last chance

during the three months of our
infantry officer basic training he caught v.d.
got arrested for pissing in public
was chased naked down the hallway
of our living quarters by someone with a knife
was thrown in jail for drunk driving
got in trouble for calling a visiting officer
from Nigeria a "darkie" at the officer's club

but the worst was the night they had us out
on maneuvers in the Georgia woods
the rain was falling so hard we wondered
why anyone would want to fight a war
while getting so wet and cold at the same time
the guys who were supposed to attack
us were smarter than we were
they never bothered to show up
so he took cover under a tree
lit up a cigarette
when lightning struck
threw him 8 ft into the air
his clothes flew off
he landed with a thud
and started running around naked
in circles as the smoke rising
from his head made him look

like a big roman candle that turned
out to be a dud

we all thought this was a message
it just wasn't meant to be
but Uncle Sam is deaf to words
like "luck" and "fate"

somewhere in Europe
he's guarding nuclear warheads

ROCK N' ROLL AUNT

i was only 5 or 6
but you used to
give me carte blanche
with your 45s and RCA
portable record player
when we came over to visit

in your room laid out
on your bed i'd listen to
the Everly Bros/Chubby Checker/
Bobby Rydell/Ritchie
Valens/Frankie Avalon
and the King whose sultry
voice made me want
to get up and move in
mysterious ways

you always knew the latest dances too
the watusi/mashed potato/the twist
on saturday nights you took
your turn strolling between
the other kids all swaying
in unison to the sounds of
Art Laboe's rock n' roll shows
and what would one day
be known as the eastside sound

your hair teased high
coy pink lips and
hypnotic maybelline eyes
the boys with dark skin
and slicked hair stood
in line for a chance
to dance with you

an angel from the
other side of the tracks

many moons have passed
now you're in icu
fading in and out
between cancer's
steady hunger and the
drugs they give you to
numb the pain
the miles between us
are many
but if i could be there
at your side
i'd thank you for planting the
seeds of teenage rebellion
in my tiny heart

whisper in your ear
how after all these years
that timeless question
of your youth will
finally be answered:

who
who
who wrote
the book of love?

IT'S A LIVING II

it's one of those days
the first call was a guy
in New York pissed off
cuz we're not gonna fill
his prescription for viagra
until his dr calls and answers
a few questions
upset with the delay
regarding his love-drug
he assumes the right to tell
me that i work for a real
"chickenshit outfit"
and that he hopes i get
the shaft one day soon

it goes downhill from there
as i start counting the minutes
until i can get up and walk
out at the end of my shift
leaving the stench of
another wasted day
hanging over my desk

and that's how it would
have been except for
the little old lady who called
to inquire about her
10 prescriptions and
the balance on her account
proceeding to tell me
about the 768 dollars
she gets every month
so she can only order
three medications at a time
staggering her refills

prioritizing them by
necessity and cost

she talks about the good
week she had collecting cans
got 18 extra bucks to
pay towards her bill

i hear her smile as she
tells me how getting
out and about keeps
her mind alert and her
joints from getting stiff

at the end of her call
she thanks me
tells me how we
do such a great job
she loves the service

later
i bring up the company website
our stock is 20 points higher
than it was 3 months ago

i was regretting not buying any
with my employee discount

but not now

Snapshot of Lorie... Davis, Illinois

i drive up to my lady's
house in the country
pulling into the gravel
driveway as storm
clouds float toward
me from the west

the breeze from the advancing
rain reminds me of the last
time a smelled a baby
fresh from the bath
pure and sweet

the only sounds are the leaves
singing back to the wind
and i'm thinking how
fortunate to be where
i am right now
when i see her
on the lawn swing
in the middle of the yard
one leg extended
the other bent
wearing white shorts riding
high on her soft thighs
a sleeveless top exposing
her graceful arms
as if posing for
a WWII pin up

tossing her head back
she flashes me her
alluring smile
points at me
whispers "come here"

our foreplay is electric
like the air around us

our lovemaking becomes the
quiet moment before
lightning strikes

"...SO EASY TO BE A POET/...SO HARD TO BE/A MAN"

FROM *40,000 FLIES* - CHARLES BUKOWKSI

late sunday night
i knew i was in trouble when my ex called
loud sad mexican songs and drunk people
yelling in the background
i can smell the cuervo on her
breath from 1300 miles away
before i can say hello
she jabs the word "asshole"
into my gut like a hot switchblade
she's just buried her father
and i know from personal experience
how a death can peel back the skin
expose those forgotten scars
and festering wounds from
another time and place

her words flew by like dirty panties
packed with rocks
i heard it all
self centered/selfish/righteous
uncaring/indignant/shameless
ungrateful/sonuvabitch

it's been awhile since i've had
the mirror held this close to my face
and i'll be the first to agree we
all need this from time to time

i almost hang up but tell
myself to be quiet and listen
it's gonna be a late night
monday morning is going
to be a bitch

but for now just
say i'm sorry
and mean it

THE WOMEN AT C.J.'S

it's always a sobering thought
to realize the music i listened to
when i was a punk doesn't even
qualify as oldie-but-goodie
but is more like jurassic park

i'm thinking about leaving
going to another bar with
a kick ass jukebox instead
of a cover band singing
"like a rolling stone" while
high on geritol and shots
of rot gut tequila

when i see them sitting
on the other side of the bar
two middle aged women
one in a pink sweater
hair short and sassy
the type i'd eventually
ask to go steady
sitting with her blonde
cheerleader friend who
wore tight skirts in class
and jumped in the backseat
at the drive-in without
being asked twice

but it's different now
they're hard and lean
bitter around the eyes
maybe a son in college who
has decided to chuck pre-law
and become a poet
maybe a daughter in high
school on the pill

maybe 2 or 3 divorces
to my one

glancing my way
i feel their search through
the pockets of my soul
looking for what i've got to
bring to the table
i feel violated
like having my underwear
drawer ransacked

it's all too much
i decide to down my beer
and make my exit

then miss pink sweater
unwraps a piece
of juicy fruit
pops it into
her pretty mouth
begins chewing the impatient
chew i've seen a
thousand times since jr. high
the chew that says
"you gonna sit there all night
talking to yourself?"

and just like that
nothing else
matters

some of them have been studying us
for many years
in awe of the way we go about
picking the carcass of our planet
like hordes of crabs on a beached whale

they were having a hard time
telling us apart
yeah, we come in different colors
and sizes but for the most part
we all looked alike to them

try it sometime...
watch ants scurrying about
their business
see what i mean?

so it was considered a stroke
of genius when one of the aliens
figured a way to identify us as individuals
while observing the humans of the
american midwest variety it was
determined that every one of us
has a different butt
no two pair of buns are alike
they photograph and catalogue us
according to wrinkles under the cheeks
bumpy jiggly cellulite surfaces
skin tight and hard
hairy or smooth
sticking out or
spread wide

the aliens have even made
our derrieres an industry
on their planet
selling coffee mugs
key chains and beautiful
lifesize posters of various
butts in natural settings

in skin-tight levi's
sitting on a barstool
in New Mexico
or hanging out a window
bare naked from a car
speeding down PCH

no alien's home would
be complete without their
famous artist's painting of
five human hineys
playing poker

so the next time you're walking
down the street or in the mall
and you feel their eyes on you
give it an exaggerated wriggle
then look over your shoulder
flash 'em a knowing wink
and a smile

then dive back into the crowd
hear them gasp in awe admiring
the gift of your elusive beauty
your gentle grace

FRIENDS II

they lived in B.F.E., Indiana
where there was no need for fences
the fields provided all the barriers
needed between neighbors
Mattie was 80 Kate was 76
and they were inseparable
Mattie drove one of those land yachts from the '70's
the ones that got 7 miles to the gallon but could hit
zero to sixty in the blink of an eye
she took Kate everywhere with her
to church, the supermarket, to get their hair done
Mattie couldn't hear and Kate couldn't see
so they complemented each other pretty well
till one day upon returning home from
a trip to the market Mattie was dropping Kate off
and forgot that Kate had to get her stuff out of the backseat
so while she was getting her groceries
Mattie stepped on it, dragging Kate under the tires
of her semi-tank, then she backed up over her friend
as she did a u-turn on the dirt road in a hurry to get
home and see Regis and Kathie Lee

the local pastor was called by the police
to approach the lady and inform her of what
she had done
they say she cried alot
gave up the keys to her car
and now stares out the window
refusing to go anywhere
at all

THE PRESIDENT SIGNS A NEW BANKRUPTCY LAW

meanwhile i'm
down to my last 20 bucks
'til payday and i allot it
accordingly to life's priorities
a 12 pack of Tecate on sale
for 8.99
a pkg of weiners
a pkg of buns
and a bag of doritos

i got a couple
of dollars left
for a rainy day or
to put towards
my retirement

this is my economic
reality

the next day i read
an article on the internet
about hot dogs being a
link to pancreatic cancer

Mr President
in lieu of this new information
and considering all the weenies
i've had to eat lately
you and Bank of America
can kiss my ass

Supporting the Troops

from the bowels of the
planet we suck dry the
slick black liquid that
keeps us humming
along

send our sons and
daughters to faraway
lands to suffer loss
of limb and life to
secure a neverending
supply

we place yellow ribbon
magnets on the backsides
of our suvs to show our
gratitude and continue
to vote like jackasses
blinded by the sun

soldiers dodging bullets
know the real score
wonder what the fuck
they're dying for

ARMY POEM IV

it's the annual "let's-see-how-
these-guys-play-war" evaluation
and we're getting our tactical asses
kicked up and down Ft. Carson
making us take a good long look
at the officer in charge

he's feeling the heat
but like every rookie coach
in the playoffs for the 1st time
he's favored by Vegas to call at
least one real boner
so when he lays out the last
battle plan it's a poet's wet dream
a cross between "Custer's Last Stand"
and "the Charge of the Light Brigade"

we all stand back
a shared glance confirming
our common agreement

for his going away present
we all chipped in and gave
him a nickel plated .45
and a bullet engraved
with his initials

FIRST KISS, 8TH GRADE, DEC. 1968

then,
it was this skinny broad cornering me
under some mistletoe,
wrapping her Olive Oyl arms around me, working
her tongue into my mouth like some sort
of persistent key.

and now,
it was the firmness of those
two small breasts pressed against my chest,
the smell of her mother's most expensive perfume,
her soft and wet tongue sliding against my teeth,
my jaws melting like hot wax.

But we did

make love in the light just once
it was our first 4th of July together
i was home alone so you picked me up
stood there in the doorway of the bathroom
watching me, shirtless, as i shaved
before we knew it we were in the
hallway in each other's arms looking
for a soft place to land

it was all a blur except for the graceful
way you extended your muscular calf
and nonchalantly flipped your ankle
sending your underwear delicately flying
across the living room

that night on the beach
your mother's suspicious looks
shot my way like a flurry of
bottle rockets while you
snuggled my head on your lap
stroked my hair
we watched one of the better displays
of fireworks i have ever seen
knowing even though it wasn't as bright
or quite as noisy
we had been there

and done that

it's a mystery to me
how i have so little
in common with my generation
no kids to put through college
no nest egg padded with soft
dreams of condos in Florida
or rustic cabins hidden deep in
the Wisconsin woods

they collect hot stocks
acquire their paper wealth
while i seek out books of poetry
search used cd stores for
vintage jazz classics
they talk about the state of
their current marriage
define themselves around soccer
schedules and seeing the latest
Disney flick

watching them become their parents
i can't help but feel i screwed up
took a left when i should have taken a right
fated to always be on
the perimeter feeling awkward
and undeveloped

but nights when i'm up 'til the wee
hours chasing the perfect poem
can feel its steamy heat brush my cheek
or when i wake up beside a beautiful woman
her gentle snore music to my ears

then it all makes sense and
i give praise to the gods

who took a liking to me
singled me out
pointed me in the direction
i was meant to take

HOW I BECAME HE-WEEPS-FIRE

I.
my post as imperial master
of night sky pictures goes back to when
i was a young man practicing my art
many said i was gifted
kissed as a child by the
venerated dragons of my ancestors
i could make a celestial canvas
black as octopus ink
light up like a thousand suns
the people loved my loud pictures
that moved and shook the walls
of the city when they exploded above

one night i showed off my
latest masterpiece
it was Bu-tan the oxen
everyone recognized him
smiled in delight as the sparks
and smoke shot out from his
flared nostrils
the thunder of the shells
rumbled through the air
many said it felt as if the beast
was actually storming the streets
and alleys

my Lord and Master
Little Storm
was only five years old then
but has often told me
on that night he knew our karma
was one
the next day i was summoned to the palace
became a member of his court

every year on my Master's birthday
i would take him up into the hills
away from the city
put on a show only for his eyes
(really... the guards had to turn
their backs and look down on the ground)
he always saw my best work first
and no matter how old he was
my sky paintings always took him back
to that mystical moment when a man
realizes some things are more important
than he will ever be
his lovely slanted eyes opened wide
pink lips shaped in a delicate "O"
soft hands clapping with each burst
of blinding light
i knew i would be with him forever

II.
in the year 7 White Swan
my Lord assumed the duties of
all powerful and benevolent ruler
he celebrated by leading an army
to the north to subdue those known
only as the barbarians-who-eat-their-
own-shit

his many victories kept me busy
i had to keep the skies
over our land filled with battle scenes
as depicted by his messengers
the people especially cheered
my version of Little Storm's javelin
projected across a starry sea of night
only to explode the head of the fierce
but stupid Asshole-Breath
leader of our new sworn enemies

my Lord defeated many armies
added riches and land to the empire
was away for many years at a time
so when his beautiful wife
my Lady Lotus-Petal began
visiting my studio to watch me work
i did whatever i was asked
quenching the thirst of her loneliness

on her birthday i created what i
considered my greatest masterpiece
to bring her honor and joy
i exploded a lotus of gunpowder and fire
the size of the moon... unfolding itself over
and over in the cool autumn night
while a river of sparks fell
gently like snow flakes from the center
and just as it seemed like
the blossoming had ended
the people were shaken by the thunderous
BOOM! and it would start all over again
my tribute lasted for over an hour
when it was finished
the sound of couples hurrying home
to recreate their own unfolding of the flower
gave the palace historians reason to
dub that night
the-time-of-many-moans

no one knew my Lord
was just outside the city gates
days ahead of his returning army
anxious to surprise Lady Lotus-Petal
later he would tell me as he watched
my display he cried for the beauty
of what it was
and how i could possibly
know it so well

as i was held down by the guards
the hot coals brushing briefly
across my eyes
i heard my Lord's voice tell me
our Lady's last breath
carried my name up to the heavens

Little Storm is most wise
he let me live
continue to work
my destiny to always see darkness
the eternal black canvas i can
never change

when i hear the crowd
ohh and ahh
the children squeal with delight
i can only cry
feel my tears falling
like the hot rain
i create so well

ANOTHER NATURE POEM

sitting at the bar
in Kelly's realizing
i'm 15 minutes away
from being stood up
when the cute redhead
across from me drinking
with her two gay guy pals
turns to slide off her stool
flashing me a glimpse of
her pink undies riding
high above the waist of
her low cut denims
but the back of the chair
has wood curving up
like a pair of dull horns
and one of them ends up
hooking the band of material
from her thong underwear
that rests in the crack of
her ass giving her what I
can only perceive as one
hell of a wedgie
i sit there watching her
struggle and realize i'm
the only one who notices

i want to reach over like
her knight in shining armor
say "allow me" and gently
practice some catch and release
when she finally wriggles her
butt frantically the way a
salmon shakes her tail

swimming upstream to
spawn and frees herself
to go pee

one class act deserves
another so when it was
clear my date was a no-show
i bought the bar a round

maybe it's me
but when sticking something
up my ass i like to know
what are the ingredients
so imagine my surprise
when flipping over the box
of Preparation H and reading
that it consists of 3% shark
liver oil

it's one thing to end up
fillet'd on some celebrity chef's
cooking show who screams
BAM as he orgasmically rubs
you down with rich aromatic
spices

there are worse ways to go
if you know what i mean
like being hunted down
chopped up and processed
as vital organs are wrung and
squeezed for the precious oils
coveted for the relief they provide
a baby boomer's itchy anal orifice

so the next time you're
on a cruise
riding the glassy surface of
a calm, romantic sea under
a full bahaman or mexican moon
holding your significant other's
hand as you snuggle on deck

making one of those memories
that will give you comfort in
your old age -

at the same moment just a
few feet below the surface
like a pack of nazi submarines
waiting for the right moment
to strike

they are watching
waiting for you to fall in
don't flatter yourself
you don't taste good
for them it's the practical
thing to do
ripping you apart
accomplishes a simple
but vital objective

making sure they have
one less asshole
in the world to
worry about

Upon Receiving a Letter from Hugh Hefner Expressing His Disappointment I'm Letting My Subscription Lapse

Hugh, while i used to covet your interviews
with guys like Miles Davis and Ralph Nader
these days i find myself not giving a rat's ass
what the rapper of the month thinks or
reading about Ben Affleck's personal
reaction upon using viagra
for the first time
and at this stage of my life
when i think of all the women
who shared my bed
i have to say i never slept with one
who came close to looking like
the ladies who grace your pages
their breasts didn't look or feel
like medicine balls
but were soft
bounced and swayed like fruit
in varied degrees of ripeness
and since any year i make 20 grand
is a good year for me
(which explains these 4 yr old jeans i'm wearing)
i think it's obvious i'll never
be able to afford the cars
or threads required to catch
the fancy of your beauties

Hugh, if your life is a sirloin
then mine is a quarter pounder
with cheese

and i can live with that
just fine

TRUER WORDS...

i'm at the Sports Page
on a Friday night
cutting loose with
some co-workers
find the nerve to break
the ice with a curvy blonde
smelling like Winston Lights
and Budweiser
she declines a dance
because she's been moving
all day into her new place
says it took a
lot out of her
uh huh whatever

but it looks promising
so before i offer to buy
a round i go to the john
with thoughts of
maybe
possible
why not
and while standing
in front of the urinal
i look up and read these
words written on the wall
at exactly eye level
as if they had been put there
just for me to see at this
crucial moment in my life:

"no matter how beautiful
she is
someone
somewhere is

sick and tired
of her shit"

pulling up my zipper
i wash my hands
head back into the crowd
remember how the gods
work and why

BABY BROTHER'S SONG OF REDEMPTION

his eyes open everyday
to epiphanies in the polluted
skies over San Gabriel Valley with
a mexican restaurant on every corner and
where high speed chases on the 605 fwy
lead to jobs paying just
enough to stay alive

he learned the hard way
to let go is an act of survival
bitter feelings should be plucked
and discarded like the weeds
choking the flowers we try to grow
in the gardens of our hearts

now he walks in grace among
the winos and meth heads
in peace with the homeless
prophets shouting their visions
of doom and salvation
the rage has subsided from
a fire out of control to the
flame of a single candle

early morning he slips
outside to the smell of
dew on summer grass
the sound of sparrow
singing thanks and praise
as a multitude of blue collar
angels rise to greet the day

standing there, alone
as God speaks his
mind for all to hear

baby brother
my enlightened one
has learned to tune in

Whimper... for Allen Ginsberg

I.

i have seen the best of my generation
selling out for a pittance of what they are worth pursuing
nike commercials and the cover of people magazine
voting for bad actors and heartless economics brutalizing
third world children so we can get a price break on denim jeans
wandering the streets avoiding eye contact avoiding touch avoiding
one another as killer STDs turn desires and needs
from spin the bottle to russian roulette
denouncing inner city crack heads and trailer park chemists caught on
law enforcement reality shows that are watched from the safety of
the homes of boob tube junkies
spending borrowed money to launch angelic armies of death
across the desert and posing prisoners in naked piles of flesh
for cell phone camera feeding frenzies
raping the forests and leaving them bruised and limp for all
to see while jerking off into ponds populated by three legged frogs
sentencing our youth to mtv lobotomy drive-by paranoias and
indentured servitude to the world banks who loan us money today
to pay off the loans of tomorrow
paying compassionate doctors to suck the fat from our hips and
inject it into our lips while burning naked under deadly solar rays trying
to look like a piece of well done meat
digging deep holes to bury atomic poisons lasting a zillion years
and hot dogs that do not decompose
filling space with satellites spying on us so government employees
looking for terrorists can watch us fuck in our bedrooms and count
how many times we say "i love you."

II.

america, we worship at the altar of Rumsfeld and burn the bones of the
dead like sticks of holy incense
america, Rumsfeld is the corporation buying votes to defeat raising
the minimum wage so the working poor will huddle in wal-mart

parking lots waiting for the doors to open
Rumsfeld! Rumsfeld's disney CEOs imprint our children with
moralistic cartoons tied in with cheap plastic action figures and
600 calorie kiddie cheesburgers
Rumsfeld is marketing genius convincing us a sneaker is
not just a sneaker
Rumsfeld is internet porn the new opiate of the people
Rumsfeld! skews his face up in contempt as young american
soldier asks for body armor to keep his nuts from being blown off
america, Rumsfeld embraces defenseless developing nations like
a drunk uncle at a family wedding who tries to slip you the tongue
Rumsfeld is our wall street global terrorist mentality our dreams to
control the markets of the world
Rumsfeld fucks america for not being able to come together for
being split divided conquered controlled me first i got mine
get yours

III.
you are gone
a soul one with
the cosmos of
Christ and Buddha
Krishna Torah and Koran
universal one
accept this
small tribute

from one lacking
the spiritual balls
to howl as loudly
as you

RACISM 101

I.
we were sitting around the tv
watching the evening news
locking our eyes on the bright
electric light the same way
our ancestors stared into
the fire under void of night

black people were marching
a lot of them
my old man scratched himself
said to know one in particular
"give them an inch and they
want a foot"

II.
first day of my first year
in a Compton school
i'm the only kid without
a black face
an aztec/mayan amongst
the children of pharoahs
never had a problem
except the one time i
got in a fight with
Sonny Williams

years later
watching Muhammad Ali
float and sting
i could say to myself
yes i know how his
opponents feel because
Sonny's small fists
were blurs smashing against

my face
pop pop pop
my only consolation
being the torn pocket
on his J.C. Penney shirt
ten minutes later
we were cowboys chasing
invisible indians

III.
my parents knew the score
and the next year
they got me in an all white
school where for the first
time i heard i too could
grow up to be the President
of the United States
the least my teacher could
have done was look at me and
say "except for you. you can't
be President." but i believed
it then and one day the first
black kid to attend our school
showed up in my class

we called him nigger
and wouldn't stand
next to him in line
he was tall and quiet
swallowed his pain
planted the seed in his heart
that would bloom into the
rage of future race riots

my mother bought me
a sweatshirt with a hood
to wear on cool days but i
hated that sweatshirt because

he had one just like it
when he hung it up in
the coat closet it hung alone
separate from the rest of
our coats and sweaters
because his clothes smelled
his clothes were dirty
his clothes were nigger clothes

i lost my sweatshirt
so it wouldn't be hung up
alone separate distant
i wanted my jacket to
hang side by side
i wanted to fit in
to grow up to be
President of the
United States

First Night... for Donna

it's the inaugural sleepover
that restless night spent
coming to terms with
a stranger in our bed
as we play tug-of-war
with the sheets
claiming then losing
territory as boundaries
expand and retreat across
the mattress with the gentle
kick of a leg or a well-timed
rolling over

we attempt to control
the various noises of
the night and hope
a certain bodily function
is kept at a minimum
as we begin to regret
that burrito we had
for lunch

thoughts of calling it off
someone going home
for the sake of a good
night's rest start to flash
through our minds

but then we find the
position we've been
looking for
becoming celestial bodies
afloat in the soft darkness

of our personal gravity
as hearts orbit each other
in perfect balance

new love pulsating like
a star in the center of
the universe we
are creating

SICK CALL II

this morning i opened my eyes
to a most extraordinary thing

her nipple
exposed
like a flower
blooming

i gazed upon it
still and silent
as the early light
gave it color
unlike any other
color in nature

with wonder
and longing
i bent my head down
gave it a soft kiss
felt its warmth
with the tip of
my tongue

after starting my day
like this
how could i possibly
want to do anything else

BROTHERS

it's our first walk together
just the two of us
his mistress/my lover
is out of town for a few days
leaving me to take care
of Jack and all his essential
needs

we pull up to the banks
of the Rio Grande damp
and humid from recent
rain with smells clinging
heavy in the air
his eyes light up
like he's finally
arrived in doggie
heaven

i open the door
his 150 lbs of rottweiler
bulk and muscle shoot
out of the car all power
and grace as his tight strung
hind legs almost rub against
each other keeping up with
the rest of his body proving
God does have a warped
sense of humor

i don't linger and walk slowly
holding hands with my lover
in her absence i quicken my pace
lengthen my stride
jog to keep up
Jack is between a

trot and a run
letting his nose read
the lay of the land

he stops to sniff a pile
of broken branches
and sticks on the ground
dried brittle crisp
letting me pass him on the trail
he gives extra attention to
smell of rabbit or lizard
calculates how big it was
the places it paused
the number of heartbeats
it needed to catch its breath
the sounds and smells that
drove it deeper into the woods

Jack catches up easily
almost knocking me down
as he brushes against my leg
his way of saying pay attention
but up ahead is another bush
demanding his pee

i take deep breathes
try to stimulate my sense
of smell and see what
he sees thru his nose
but it's no contest

back at the car i pull
out the plastic container
of water and watch him
as if he's found life's greatest joy
lapping it up likes it's the
best thing he's ever touched
with his tongue

here's to the dogs we meet in life
the ones who step aside and
let us share their turf
the ones who let us run
alongside while tolerating
our bumbling ineptitudes
the ones who accept us
for what we are

i'd often experienced your endless patience
but never your swift justice, until one day
Uncle Chuy was driving the station wagon down the 605 freeway
and you had your hands full
the baby was up front with you and we were in the back
raising hell, your four sons and your favorite nephew
you kept telling us to behave but it was summer
we were out of school and i was going to be visiting for the next two weeks
we were plotting our itinerary... could we possibly top last year when
we each blew up a roll of caps simultaneously? till this day i still laugh when
i recall how the neighbor's cat jumped into the air and shit at the same time

so when you told us to behave for the last time
we didn't hear you, and before anyone could yell "duck!"
your hand came over the seat wielding your shoe like a grotesque
Cecil or Lambchop from hell, and with the kind of sound effects
reserved for a Three Stooges movie i heard the thud of leather
as you made contact with every skull within reach except mine
('cause i am your favorite nephew, thank God)
i felt bad for my cousins, tearfully rubbing their heads
and sitting still for the rest of the ride
but when they knew you weren't looking in the rearview mirror
to my surprise they grinned, threw me a wink and gave me thumbs up

our summer could only go uphill from there

DRIVING TO O'HARE

both are in the backseat
my mother-in-law and her comadre
going back to California for a funeral
it was kind of like Driving Miss Daisy times two
but this is my good deed for the month
and i feel alright about it
they have their rituals
while behind the driver's wheel i hear the unsnapping
of wallets, the sound of unfolding plastic
as they bring out their pictures
play each one like a card in a game of poker
"this is Lori, Sandy's daughter, she graduated from...
she is a... she makes x amount a year... her husband
is going to teach... they bought a new house."
"how nice... she looks like Sandy... this is Chuckie... Tommy's
oldest... he owns a contsruction company... he built me a new
kitchen.... these are his kids... this one gets all A's."
they do this for quite awhile until they realize
they've both been around long enough not to be
able to outdo the other
they begin to talk about the good old days
mom worked in the factory that made uniforms
for the soldiers who fought WWII
her friend worked where they made ammunition cases
mom joined the army and would stand on the runway
giving hand signals to the pilots
helping them park their planes
her friend worked in a foundry making parts for tanks
mom was a real live Rosie the Riveter
driving fasteners into the wings of brand new airplanes

finally they begin to laugh
both agreeing it's been one hell of a ride
but well worth it
and i take a look in the rearview mirror
humbled by my precious cargo

he's over 70 yrs old
and we're going to Platteville
the Bears are scrimmaging the Browns
and i know he's getting cabin fever
so when i call him up and invite him
he jumps
we leave early, the morning fog clinging to
everything around us
and he's talking, pointing out backroads
he's explored in his prime with some of the
local farmers' daughters
"there used to be a factory there"
or "they make good cheese here"
he talks of his wife who is always in a hurry
to get somewhere, while he likes to take
his time, wander up the hidden alley or drive
down the nameless road
(now i know why he grins when she tells
everyone who will listen how he constantly
gets lost)
i hear about WWII, a young sailor holding his dead buddy
in disbelief in the middle of battle, and docking
in South America and instead of hitting the local
cantinas and whorehouses he went deep into the
jungle and found a watering hole where he tasted
the native brew
(i magine him now at the VFW, laughing with his
friends and spending his pension freely, buying
drinks and tipping big)
he talks of waking up the day after his mother died
when he was only seven and finding another woman
in his father's bed
he left, ran away on the trains, rode them from Tejas
to Louisiana, then north to Freeport, Illinois
some people took him in, raised him like one of their own

approaching a slight incline up ahead
he points, "i used to make friends with
the illegals that the farmers used to hire
and i would bring them to the top of this hill
and show them the view," and sure enough
as we crest the hill i take in scenery fit for postcards
the lush green of the growing corn
covering the rolling hills flushes my cheeks
i roll down the window and smell the scent of cows
and the approaching afternoon storm
i can only imagine the awe of those men
from Mexico seeing land so fertile all they had
to do was throw the seed in the air and it would
grow wherever it landed

so today i thank you, Armando
for adding me to the list of men you saw fit
to share your view
gracias viejo
mi amigo

ARMY POEM V

it was my turn to entertain our visiting officer from the Philippines
he'd been taken to the theater/a theme park/a picnic/someone
even dragged him to church/so when they turned him over to me
the bachelor lieutenant from LA./we did what soldiers in a strange
town always do/we found a good topless bar/the main attraction
was Morgana the Kissing Bandit/made her rep running onto the fields
of professional baseball games and planting a smooch on her favorite
player/she always got a standing ovation as the cops escorted her out
of the park/her 60 plus inches of breasts bouncing like two fumbled
footballs any guy in the stands would have gladly tried to recover

so she was on stage and when her top came off the grin on my friend's
face told me he was finally seeing the promised land/she took
two hats from the audience and twirled them on the tips
of her hard nipples like mini hula hoops/
we ordered another round and i tipped Morgana
a twenty/she came over and gave my guest a kiss on the cheek/

Morgana/my dear/this is to say
while many would not consider you
a suitable substitute for all the opportunity
and dysfunction this country stands for/
Lady Liberty was nowhere in sight/and
you filled in just fine

ABOUT THE AUTHOR

RICHARD VARGAS was born and raised in Southern California. He graduated from Cal State University, Long Beach. He edited/published a small
press poetry magazine, *The Tequila Review,* from 1977-1979. Various jobs
throughout the years include: fry cook, the guy who used to fill your gas
tank and check your oil, warehouseman, delivery man, bank clerk,
women's shoe salesman, infantry officer, UPS man, massage therapist,
bookseller, community relations manager, distribution supervisor,
inbound call center customer service. Poems have been published in
The Wormwood Review, Rattle, Main Street Rag, Blue Mesa Review, Willow Review,
Rockford Review, Java Snob, Eros, Breakfast All Day (U.K.), Bilingual Review/
Bilinque Revista, Chiron Review, and others. His first collection of poetry,
McLife, was published Fall 2005 by Main Street Rag Press, and poems
from the book have been featured on Garrison Keillor's Writer's
Almanac. He's currently enrolled in the MFA/Creative Writing
Program at the University of New Mexico and welcomes comments
at picodegallo54@yahoo.com